Wisdom and Number

WISDOM and NUMBER

Toward a Critical Appraisal of the
Middle English Religious Lyric

STEPHEN MANNING

*The soul truly becomes better . . . when it
turns away from the carnal senses and is re-
formed by the divine numbers of wisdom. For
thus it is said in Holy Scripture: "I have made
the circuit in order to know and contemplate
and seek wisdom and number."*
—*St. Augustine,* De Musica, *VI.iv.7*

UNIVERSITY OF NEBRASKA PRESS · *Lincoln* · 1962

Publishers on the Plains

UNP

THE PUBLICATION OF THIS BOOK WAS ASSISTED BY
A GRANT FROM THE FORD FOUNDATION.

821.1
M284

44897

TO MY PARENTS

PREFACE

If we accept the catalogue of faults which some commentators level against the Middle English religious lyrics, we can immediately sentence these poems to a circle in some aesthetic inferno and turn our attention to other literary matters. For—item—the problems which these lyrics raise are more theological than literary. And —item—we modern readers can find little relevance in a theology constructed upon an alien, if not outmoded, system of beliefs. Item. The religious subject matter actually fettered the talents of the lyrists, and we may marvel that any good religious lyrics came out of England at all. Item. The lyrics are flat. They do not produce a tremolo with arrowlike flight straight from the heart. These charges point out, in effect, that the religious lyrics have no significant theological, emotional, or literary value.[1] And we shall probably agree to these charges if we try to read the lyrics as sermons, or if we insist upon evaluating them as though they had been written by Romantic or modern poets. Of course the lyrics are disappointing and do not invite rereading if we expect to push aside the diction and find an author carrying his heart in his hands. Significantly enough, these poems were not written in anticipation of modern preconceptions about the lyric. They are *songs*. And they must be judged as such.

As songs, the religious lyrics bear strengths and

weaknesses and potentialities of which commentators
have been only partially aware. One critic has remarked
that

> The characteristics suggested for the song lyric make it un-
> likely that . . . [these] lyrics will give much reward to the
> seeker after deep and original thought, subtle psychology,
> strange imagery, or social or philosophical implications in
> literature. In fact, these lyrics are notorious for their
> repetitive subject-matter . . . , their well-worn imagery
> and their light intellectual weight.

Such a judgment seems to sum up very neatly a reason-
able attitude toward the Middle English religious lyric,
but the critic is Catherine Ing, and her subject is the
Elizabethan lyric.[2] Yet she argues for the merits of
Elizabethan songs on purely literary grounds; might we
not therefore do the same for the medieval songs?

When we approach these songs we must remember
that they concern themselves more with eliciting emotional response (for spiritual purposes) than with describing or analyzing emotional experience on the assumption that the experience is valuable in and of itself.
The speaker in these religious songs ordinarily does not
present his thought, feeling, or emotion as an intense
experience which he at this moment undergoes; rather
he places his audience between himself and his experience and merely reports it in terms which his audience
associates with that experience. His medieval audience
placed the value of the sung experience more in the
subject matter itself than in the experiencing of it. The
speaker had merely to confirm that value. Thus the
myopic charges which commentators have brought against
the lyrics at least squint at three basic problems. First,
if we are to judge the literary value of these songs, we
must determine the criterion for evaluating the relationship between the religious subject matter and the literary
form of the song. Second, we must determine the worth
of the lyric situation in these songs, and the value of

the corresponding emotive structure. Finally, we must determine what particular literary qualities give the songs their particular literary value. One solution to the last problem should be obvious—the literary worth of these poems must lie in just those qualities which make them songs: devices of sound. This answer suggests immediately an answer to the preceding problem: since the song generally cannot develop the characterization of the speaker as fully as does the modern dramatic lyric, its lyric situation is not the basis of its emotive power. The song depends more for its emotional response upon that which makes it a song: its use of sound. The solution to the first problem is more complex, but we may easily see its general outline. The religious subject matter is most satisfactorily handled when the poet does not merely invite his reader to accept the value of the given experience, but rather stresses its value so that his audience can contemplate and somehow penetrate the meaning of that experience. On the other hand, when the poet chooses merely to confirm the inherent value of the experience, he may yet handle his subject satisfactorily if, in treating it with less perception than emotion, he skilfully manipulates the sound. The fact that the religious subject matter is inherently charged with feeling and significance means that the poet must steer carefully between overemphasizing the implicit emotion, thereby sinking to bathos, and taking the value of his subject so much for granted that he presents the experience without even suggesting its emotive force.

The fact that almost all medieval religious lyrics are songs thus determines the handling of both the religious subject matter and the lyric situation, and consequently determines their literary value. In the chapters which follow I shall attempt to demonstrate the dependence of these three qualities upon the form of the song. In the first chapter I shall discuss the role which sound plays in the lyrics, and point out three generally used patterns which structure the sound of the lyrics. In the second chapter I shall compare the lyric situation in the song and in the dramatic lyric, analyzing the three chief *personae* that the lyrists assume. Then, since these are religious songs, I shall examine their handling of three aspects of the tradition of religious literature: devotional forms, imagery, and wit. Each of these aspects points directly to the nature of the lyrics as songs. First, the song tends to have a loose thought structure. We must therefore inquire what, if any, are the structures which do bind it together, and what are the criteria we should use to evaluate the comparative success or failure in employing a loose structure. Second, the song tends toward clichés. We must therefore inquire what kinds of images it uses, how well it uses them, and to what extent the imagery itself structures the poem. Third, the song stresses sound, often at the expense of the thought. We must therefore inquire whether it can possess any intellectual content at all.

The discussion of the lyrics which follows is, I hope, one more step toward a judicious critical appraisal of this important group of poems. I have generally ignored the historical vagaries of the lyrics, bringing in historical considerations only when these pertain directly to the literary matters at hand. I have tried, however, to combine close textual analysis with as much of the cultural background as I have found necessary for an accurate description and evaluation of the literary achievement. Whenever possible, I cite parallels in English authors. I have accepted the texts which editors have already provided, drawing heavily from Brown's three anthologies and Greene's collection of carols, but I have not hesitated to repunctuate according to my own tastes. Finally, since I am not writing for the specialist in Middle English, I have glossed the texts wherever I thought such glosses would prove helpful to the reader who is not at ease with the language.

At this point I make the customary acknowledgments, but with as keen a sense of appreciation as an author can express: to the Council on Research and Creative Work of the University of Colorado for a Faculty Fellowship and financial assistance; to the Committee on Research of the University of Virginia for assistance in having the manuscript typed; to Mrs. Eloise Pearson, not the least for making sense out of the manuscript when no sense was there; to my colleagues, especially Robert L. Kellogg; to the University of Nebraska Press and its readers, especially Paul A. Olson, whose suggestions and many kindnesses I particularly appreciate; to Professor Kemp Malone, who aroused and directed my first interest in the religious lyrics.

1. Cf. such views as the following: Kane (p. 179) contends that "the religious subject as a whole had a restrictive effect upon its poets"; Brook (p. 16) reduces the "most interesting feature" of the lyrics to "the way in which they have been influenced by the phraseology of love lyrics"; John Speirs, *Medieval English Poetry* (London, 1957), p. 49, claims that if we discover which of the Middle English lyrics still mean "something significant" today, we are "left with only a few poems"; Gangacharan Kar, *Thoughts on the Mediaeval Lyric* (London, 1933), p. 20, feels that some of the lyrics

> have a simple, little heart, bearing all things, believing all things, hoping all things and enduring all things. Others are puffed up, and though they develop one whole new limb, namely, the knowing hand, they forget the use of the heart;

and Arthur K. Moore, *The Secular Lyric in Middle English* (Lexington, 1951), p. vii, contends that

> the typical questions raised by the religious lyric are more theological than literary and fall therefore on the fringes of criticism. But the need for study in this direction I do not for one moment deny. I do hazard the judgment, however, that on the basis of intrinsic merit the secular lyrics are more deserving of notice than the religious.

Finally, the lyrics' dullness and lack of aesthetic merit were two of the points of Rossell Hope Robbins' paper, "What's to Be Done with the Lyric," read before the English 2 section of the MLA meeting December 29, 1960.

2. *Elizabethan Lyrics* (London, 1951), p. 20.

CONTENTS

PREFACE   vii

ABBREVIATIONS   2

CHAPTER ONE: *The Lyrics as Songs*   3

CHAPTER TWO: *The Lyric Situation*   35

CHAPTER THREE: *Some Religious Structures*   56

CHAPTER FOUR: *Analogy and Imagery*   90

CHAPTER FIVE: *Piety and Wit*   138

CONCLUSION   171

APPENDIX   177

INDEX OF POEMS AND AUTHORS   187

INDEX OF PRINCIPAL TOPICS   193

Wisdom and Number

ABBREVIATIONS USED IN THIS STUDY:

XIII   Brown, Carleton, ed. *English Lyrics of the XIIIth Century*. Oxford, 1932.*

XIV   Brown, Carleton, ed. *Religious Lyrics of the XIVth Century*, 2nd ed., rev. G. V. Smithers. Oxford, 1952.*

XV   Brown, Carleton, ed. *Religious Lyrics of the XVth Century*. Oxford, 1939.*

AH   *Analecta Hymnica*. Ed. Guido Dreves and Clemens Blume. Leipzig, 1886–1922.

Brook   Brook, G. L. *The Harley Lyrics*, 2nd ed. Manchester, 1956.

Greene   Greene, Richard, ed. *The Early English Carols*. Oxford, 1935.*

Kane   Kane, George. *Middle English Literature*. London, 1951.

Patterson   Patterson, Frank Allen. *The Middle English Penitential Lyric*. New York, 1911.

PG   *Patrologia Graeca*. Ed. J. P. Migne. Paris, 1886–1912.

PL   *Patrologia Latina*. Ed. J. P. Migne. Paris, 1842–80.

* Texts are here reprinted with the permission of the Oxford University Press.

CHAPTER ONE

THE LYRICS AS SONGS

The two types of lyrics which I have distinguished —the song and the intensely personal or dramatic lyric —differ from each other in the attention they pay to their sound, and in the degree to which they utilize their lyric situation. This chapter examines the role of the sound. The song, on the one hand, exhibits a regular meter and accents its rime; the dramatic lyric, on the other hand, exhibits frequent metrical irregularities and favors enjambement; the respective difference corresponds to what Northrop Frye has called the emotional and the technical qualities of music in poetry. The former "sounds nice" because the poet pleasantly varies his vowel sounds and avoids the harsher consonant clusters; the latter, however, shares in "the tension and the driving accented impetus of music." [1] Some critics have justly found the religious lyrics "charming," for, as Frye says, the root of the musical element in the lyric is the charm, "the hypnotic incantation that, through its pulsating dance rhythm, appeals to involuntary physical response." At one extreme the sound pattern of the song looms so conspicuous that it hypnotizes the reader, who becomes involved in the pulsating rhythm and barely attends the meaning of the words. He detects a recurrence of individual sounds, of words, and of larger structures; he actually anticipates their recurrence, and when his expectation is fulfilled, experiences a particularly pleasurable response. By *song*, then, I do not mean a lyric set to music. I mean every poem whose sound pattern creates something of a hypnotic effect. Such a lyric elicits its characteristic agreeable response—"sounding nice"—by relying heavily on meter, rime, and rhythm. The meter pleases when it is conspicuous and when, after being varied, it resumes its regularity. Rime satisfies when the listener can detect the recurrence of the vowel sound. According to Henry Lanz, as soon as we hear a second vowel sound, we develop a strong impulse to return to the original sound. The poet may gratify this impulse either by returning directly to the same vowel, or by returning only after using other vowel sounds. The latter technique adds a feeling of suspense to the original impulse, and enhances the satisfaction of having the expectation fulfilled.[2] Thus, a rime scheme of a b a b creates a different response than does a a a a.* The pleasure which rime gives, then, arises from its frequency, its patterning (especially a cross-patterning), and the variations in line length (which will increase or decrease attention to the rime). Rhythm also determines the musical quality of the song by such devices as the variation of speed within each line, by the repetition and variation of patterns in speed from line to line and from stanza to stanza, by the variations in cadence within each line (rising, falling, neutral), and by the repetition of cadence patterns throughout the stanza. When these

* The effectiveness of withholding the rime vowel is very clearly seen in "At a sprynge wel vnder a þorn" (XIV, No. 130). The rime scheme begins with a a, then shifts to b c, so that the reader's expectation of b b is not fulfilled. He then anticipates the recurrence of either b or c; the fifth line is d, so that the return to c in the last line is particularly gratifying.

three factors, then—rhythm, rime, meter—are accented in a poem so that the total effect is almost hypnotic, the lyric is a song.

Since most medieval religious lyrics are songs, any attempt at literary appraisal must include some remarks on their characteristic sound patterns. To get at the essential character of the prosody of the song, let us consider the sound of the following stanza (XIV, No. 66):

> Loue me brouthte   *brought*
> & loue me wrouthte,
>   Man, to be þi fere.   *companion*
> 4 Loue me fedde,
> & loue me ledde,
>   & loue me lettet here.   *abandons*

Within this simple stanza form the poet has handled his sound skilfully. To prevent the sound from galloping away with the thought, he varies his meter; in fact, he does not establish his meter definitely until the final two lines of the stanza. Here we find perfect regularity where before we found variation, and the definite emergence of the meter at the end pleases us because it creates a sense of perfect order. The poet employs other devices as well to solve a problem inherent in the song—to strike the necessary balance between too much sound and too much sense. By withholding his b rime, he arouses our expectation, then satisfies it in line 6. He calls attention to these lines also by adding a third stress. Moreover, he varies his pattern of anaphora: lines 1 and 4 alternate with lines 2 and 5. He breaks this pattern in line 3, but instead of repeating the break, makes line 6 repeat line 5. Finally, he strengthens his sound with balance, alliteration, and assonance. As the poem proceeds, however, the author emphasizes his sound less and less, apparently wishing to prevent his poem from becoming too hypnotic at the expense of the thought. The pattern he established in the last three lines of stanza

one reappears in the first three lines of stanza two, even
to the repetition of the b rime. But in the next three
lines (10–12) he drops his parallelism and anaphora, and
he does not pick it up in the final stanza. Although we
still hear a strong, but modified, sound pattern, we become more directly aware of the meaning of the words.
All the devices of sound have combined to create a rapid
tempo; so lighthearted a tone as this sound creates is
justified by the content of the last three lines of the poem:

> 16   to hauen þe,
>   Wel is me,
>   I haue þe wonnen in fith.   *fight*

The Christ of this poem thus views His sufferings, as in
Juliana of Norwich, with "glad cheer"; [3] the sound intensifies the inherent value of this religious subject matter.

The balance between sound and sense is a particularly bothersome problem of the song lyric; the audience's attention to sound seems necessarily to reduce its
attention to thought. At one extreme, the song may
almost completely subject the thought to the metrical
regularity and other features of the sound pattern. In
less extreme examples, the song may so relate sound and
sense that the sound structure buttresses the sense, but
in such examples we cannot easily be dogmatic. While
the poet of "Loue me brouthte" hushes the regularity
of his meter to focus his subject, the poet of "Adam lay
I-bowndyn" (XV, No. 83) exacts this very quality from
his meter precisely because he has penetrated the significance of his topic:

> Adam lay I-bowndyn,
>   bowndyn in a bond;
> fowre þowsand wynter
> 4   þowt he not to long;
> And al was for an appil,
>   an appil þat he tok,

As clerkis fyndyn
8   wretyn in here book.
Ne hadde þe appil take ben,
       þe appil taken ben,
ne hadde neuer our lady
12   a ben heuene qwen.
Blyssid be þe tyme
       þat appil take was—
Þer-fore we mown syngyn,
16   "Deo gracias!"

The poem explodes with joy in both the thought and sound patterns. The poet suggests his tone in line 4, thereby placing the apparent insignificance of the apple in line 5 in its proper theological context; he suggests his tone again in the contrast between the clerks of line 7 and *we* of line 15. Clerks are for finding the causes of such matters, the speaker seems to say; we, however, are concerned more with the effects, and we can sing for joy. Moreover, the tight logic with which the poet fashions his variation of the *felix culpa* motif establishes the basis for the joy, and the meter so insists on it, that the listener shares the emotion. In fact, lines 7–8 and 12 have to be squeezed into the meter, to be syncopated as it were,[4] yet this is precisely what the poem demands. For the strong beat supports the sense of joy; it may even be connected with some kind of dance movement, for the repetition of *bowndyn,** appil,* and *appil* in lines 2, 6, and 10 creates the impression of stepping forward, then backward, then forward again. Thus, although the technique in this lyric differs from that in "Loue me brouthte," the sound in both poems intensifies the poets' insights into their religious subject matter.

Placing too much pressure on the musical effects of the song can sometimes lead to inconsistencies or inco-

---

* This repetition heightens the variation in the vowel sound at the end of line 2: *bowndyn, bowndyn,* then *bond.*

herences in the thought, which, however, the sound can smooth over. Just as mothers can charm their babies to sleep with nonsense phrases, so the sound pattern of a song can lull the listener to the point that the inconsistencies and incoherences slip by unheeded. For example, in the opening stanza of a familiar Marian lyric, the sound pattern dominates the grammatical structure (XIII, No. 17B):

> Of on þat is so fayr and briȝt   *one*   *bright*
>   velud maris stella,
> Briȝter þan þe day-is liȝt,
> 4   parens & puella;
> Ic crie to þe, þou se to me;
> Leuedy, preye þi sone for me,
>   tam pia,
> 8   þat ic mote come to þe,
>   maria.

As commentators have pronounced, the lyric is charming. The engaging sound effects arise partly from the conflict between a rising and a falling rhythm, and partly from the interplay of vowel and consonant combinations.* However, lines 1–4 comprise a long prepositional phrase which modifies nothing, and has only the vaguest relationship with lines 5–9. But the fact that they do not make perfect grammatical sense does not detract from their charm one whit. The listener automatically lets the sound pattern so sway him that he is only half aware

---

* Line 2 reverses the direction of line 1 from rising to falling; the conflict thus set up resolves tentatively in line 7 and finally in line 9 into a neutral cadence. The resolution rises naturally from lines 2 and 4, for lines 7 and 9 repeat the meter of the last three syllables of these other Latin lines. Part of the charm stems also from the interplay of vowel sounds in the first four lines: the rime word at the end of line 1 is echoed at the beginning and end of line 3; the *el* sound in line 2 appears at both beginning and end (*vel*ud, ste*ll*a); and lines 2 and 4 repeat two rimes (*mar*is ste*ll*a and *par*ens, pue*ll*a).

of the thought pattern anyway. This stanza therefore illustrates in the lyric the effect which Suzanne Langer finds in songs which are sung: "Words may enter directly into musical structure even without being literally understood; the *semblance of speech* may be enough." [5] This special blend of sound and sense, however, is not merely one of the lyric's most enchanting qualities; it is one of its most Circean.

Now while in the song the sound pattern calls attention to itself so that it almost hypnotizes the reader, in the dramatic lyric the sound dances attendance on the thought. The dramatic lyric does not reach for hypnotic effects; its sound may even contain discordant elements. It seeks instead to approximate the vagaries of actual speech rhythms and invites attention to the meaning of its words. Moreover, the emotive pattern of the dramatic lyric will tend to be more complex than that of the song: while the song tends to rely upon sound alone to convey the desired emotional effects, the dramatic lyric counts on a combination of such elements as sound, diction (especially imagery), and full exploitation of the lyric situation to produce its emotional impact. Although some medieval lyrics contain elements which suggest the techniques of the dramatic lyric, they do not approach that degree of dramatic intensity which Robert Langbaum has labelled "the poetry of experience." [6] At their most dramatic, the religious lyrics merely straddle the boundary between the two types. For example, in the following lines we can hear the rhythm of the dramatic voice (XV, No. 98):

> O Ihesu, lett me neuer forgett thy byttur pas-
>   sion
> That thou suffred for my transgression,
> ffor in thy blessyd wondes is the verey scole
> 4 That must teche me with the worlde to be
>   called a fole.

O Ihesu, ihesu, ihesu, grauntt that I may loue
    the soo
Þat the wysdom of the worlde be cleene fro me
    A-goo,
And brennyngly to desyre to come to see thy
    face,
8   In whom is all my comford, my joy, and my
    solace.

The rhythm of this poem creates an impression of actual
speech rhythms primarily because it varies the number
of stressed syllables per line (especially lines 1–2, 5), and
because it distributes its pauses as actual speech might
distribute them (lines 5, 8; the use of enjambement).
The sound in general reinforces the emotive structure;
the long lines capture the meditative tone of the whole.
The pauses in line 5 intensify its appeal, as does its
contrast with line 1, where the addressee is named only
once. The pauses in line 8 slow down its movement; the
line thus suggests the attainment of the desired goal, or
at least the calm which such attainment would bring.
The tone fluctuates between an intensity and a calm,
corresponding to the speaker's emotional experience.
At times the irregularity of the metrical pattern in the
semidramatic lyric appears in the interchange of stanzas
with a variable number of stresses per line; "Leuedi
sainte marie, moder and meide" (XIII, No. 2) employs
stanzas of both six and seven stresses per line, although
the alternation of these two stanza forms shows no over-
all pattern. Moreover, an occasional line within the stanza
varies from the norm.* When the song lyric utilizes this
same basic technique of variation in stanza forms, it
tends toward a patterning in the variation; this pattern
sometimes shows up in the phrasing: the pauses tend to
fall in identical places from stanza to stanza. In "Leuedi
sainte marie," however, the tendency toward a medial

* E.g., lines 14, 25.

caesura (after the third or fourth stress) varies. Irregularity in the song still makes the song sing; irregularity in the dramatic lyric makes it converse.

Many of the religious songs sing not only because of their prosody, but also because they were actually set to music. A number of them have come down to us with their original notation, and others are incorporated into what seem to be minstrel collections.[7] To gauge the influence of this music on prosody at all accurately is difficult on the basis of the surviving examples. In most of these, the stanza form and the melody have nothing in common, so that exploring the relationship between the two is not as helpful as it might at first seem.* Hence, in the discussion which follows, I am interested in the direct influence of music only when it does seem to affect the literary quality of the poems; to consider them as songs in a musical sense lies outside my scope. However, two aspects of the relationship between music and verse are relevant here. First of all, the modern reader should be alert to the possibility that what he finds discordant in a given lyric may not have been discordant to the poet or his audience. The elaborate system of polyphony which medieval England developed may similarly strike the modern listener as cacophonous. Simple irregularities in the lyrics can often be explained on the basis of the relationship between words and music;

---

* Sometimes the two do correspond, as in the rondel, where the poetic refrain corresponds to a musical refrain ("Ihesu, þat al þis world haþ wroʒt," XIV, No. 35 has this form); the prosa, where the irregularity of the stanza form is matched by the melodic structure (one lyric which vaguely approximates this form is "þe fader of heuene," XV, No. 84); sometimes in the sequence, where the last three lines have a rime scheme which echoes the first three (a a b c c b), and the corresponding melody echoes or repeats the first three lines (an example of the sequence form is "Stond wel, moder, vnder rode," XIII, No. 49B). On the other hand, so complex a form as the isorhythmic motet, where the melody overlaps a definite rhythmical pattern, exhibits none of this complexity in the words.

if a line has too many syllables, or too few, the resulting "discord" in the sound pattern may not appear at all when the words are sung. Then too, the medievals were more accustomed to large numbers of unstressed syllables in the classic form of alliterative poetry, and in Gregorian psalmody as well, where accent yields to a formula of, generally, four stresses.[8] A further observation about the relationship between music and verse: the sound pattern of the verse is analogous to the music of an actual song. Now, words which are set to music are often so nondescript that the music must carry the emotional burden. Similarly, the words of a song lyric are often equally colorless, and the sound pattern must create, practically of itself, the poem's emotional or imaginative intensity. In "The fyrst day wan Crist was borne" (Greene, No. 41), for example, a note of joy sounds immediately in the burden: "Nowel, el, el, el, el! / I thank it a maydyn euery del." The details in the individual stanzas, however, do not lend themselves at first glance to a note of joy, yet the meter moves too swiftly to support any other tone:

Tho the peler he was bow[n]dyn;	*To*
Tho his hart a sper was stunggyn;	*through*
For us he sofered a deadly wondyn;	
20 I thanke it a maydyn euery dyll.	*bit*

In this poem the speaker looks upon the Passion and death of Christ, not with the sorrow with which they are usually viewed, but with the joy which recognizes their salutary effects, and which also recognizes Mary's role in redemption. Since the song lyric may thus depend primarily upon its sound pattern for its emotional intensity, an important corollary follows: if the sound pattern is skilfully handled, it can compensate for weaknesses in the thought pattern, in the diction, and in the characterization of the speaker.

When we turn to the sound patterns themselves, we

can detect three kinds of structure which occur widely; for convenience I shall call them linear, monostrophic, and polystrophic. When the structure of sound is linear, the line, rather than the stanza, displays the basic sound pattern. When the structure is monostrophic, the same stanza form appears throughout the poem; when it is polystrophic, the stanza forms vary in length, meter, and/or rime scheme. Since linear structure refers to the composition of the individual stanza, and since the other two structures refer to the structural relationships between stanzas, a given poem may utilize both linear and either monostrophic or polystrophic structure. Each of these structures creates a musical pattern; each can be used to reinforce or obscure the thought of the poem. How they are so used in individual poems will be our concern.

Linear structure allows for a number of variations. We can find the single line and the couplet as the basic unit; we can find what we might call a monodic and a polyphonic use of the single line; we can find the single line unit combined with polystrophic structure. "Þe minde of þi passiun" (XIII, No. 56A) makes striking use of the single line as the basic sound unit:

Þe minde of þi passiun, suete ihesu— *contemplation*
  þe teres it tollid,   *drew forth*
  þe heine it bolled;   *eyes swelled*
4 þe neb it wetth,   *face*
  in herte sueteth.

The poem as a whole is fragmentary, as though the experience itself were so ineffable that it could be expressed only in fragments. The abrupt opening suggests an intensity which calms in the regularity of the next four lines; thus the calm which accompanies the sweetening of the heart is suggested by the cumulative effect of the linear structure. This structure breaks in half with the break in rime scheme; and the breach in sound corresponds to a breach in thought. Rather than reading the first two verbs as present tense and therefore parallel with the last two (as Brown does), we give the poem a greater sense of urgency if we read them as past tense. Such a reading invests the couplet with the fragmentary quality of the opening line. The speaker has so vividly recalled the grief of perhaps those standing about the cross that he actually participates in their sorrow. Theirs is the measure of his, for such is the power of the contemplation of Christ's suffering now as then. Yet, paradoxically, the contemplation is so intense that it merges pain and pleasure, for the speaker has penetrated the meaning of Christ's suffering.[9] The final line, the emotional climax, is reinforced by its variation in the linear structure. The sound has thus supported the sense, focused it, modulated it.

Linear structure may also set to work a larger, two-line unit, as in "Kyndeli is now mi coming" (XIV, No. 53), which approximates the musical form of the *descort*.[10] In each couplet the first line parallels grammatically the first line of the other couplets. The linear structure, however, depends less upon the grammatical arrangement than upon the metrical pattern and rime scheme.

> Kyndeli is now mi coming   *according to nature*
> in to ȝis [werld] wiht teres and cry;
> Litel and pouere is myn hauing,
> 4 briȝel and sone i-falle from hi;   *frail*
> Scharp and strong is mi deying,
> i ne woth whider schal i;   *know*
> Fowl and stinkande is mi roting—
> 8 on me, ihesu, ȝow haue mercy.   *you*

The basic linear unit consists of a four-stress line ending in an unaccented *-ing* and a second four-stress line ending in an *i* rime. The fact that the couplet does not rime makes us anticipate the recurrence of the *i* sound; when we hear it, we are gratified. The fourfold occurrence of this pattern suggests a sense of continuity, of repetition—

a sense which reinforces the impression in the thought
pattern of a cyclical movement in life. The fact that
the members of the couplet do not rime with one another
also creates a sense of deliberateness and inevitability—
a sense which sustains similar qualities in the speaker's
attitude towards life. But the tone created by the sound
pattern arises also from the alternation of a rising and
falling cadence in the first and second lines respectively
of each couplet. The alternation is not exact (although
I would like to make it so, for this is the principle of the
descort). The last two lines do exemplify perfect alternation:

$$/ \text{ x } / \text{ x } / \text{ x } / \text{ x}$$
$$\text{x } / \text{ x } / \text{ x } / \text{ x } /$$

Most of the remaining lines can be encouraged to fall
into this pattern, except lines 5–6, which vary the
pattern:

$$/ \text{ x } / \text{ ( ) } / \text{ x } / \text{ x}$$
$$\text{( ) } / \text{ x } / / \text{ x x } /$$

Though the resemblance to the *descort* here is close
enough to be striking, what matters from a literary point
of view is that a conflict is set up between a falling and
rising cadence; this conflict suggests in this poem the
tribulations of life of which the thought pattern speaks.
The total effect of the sound verifies emotionally a fact
which the medieval audience took for granted.

   Two other poems which exhibit linear structure
share the same subject matter—the signs of death. Taken
together, they demonstrate how variations with the same
sound pattern can embellish differently the same topic.
The first of these poems has what we might call a simple,
monodic structure (XIII, No. 71):

> Wanne mine eyhnen misten,   *eyes*
> and mine heren sissen,   *ears cease*
> and mine nose koldet,

4   and mine tunge ffoldet,
         and mi rude slaket,   *complexion is impaired*
         And mine lippes blaken,
         and mi muþ grennet,   *grimaces*
8   and mi spotel rennet,
         and mi her riset,
         and min herte griset,   *trembles*
         and mine honden biuien,   *quiver*
12   and mine ffet stiuien—   *stiffen*
         al to late, al to late,
         wanne þe bere ys ate gate!   *bier*
         Þanne ye schel fflutte   *go*
16   ffrom bedde te fflore,
         ffrom fflore to here,   *shroud*
         ffrom here to bere,
         ffrom bere to putte,   *pit*
20   and te putt ffor-dut.   *shut up*
         þanne lyd min hus vppe min   *then when my*
            nose,   *house lies upon my nose*
         off al þis world ne gyffe ihic a   *give I a pea*
            pese.

When we finish reading this poem, we have a fairly good idea about the condition of man's body at death; the horrifying effect of the first twelve lines depends upon both the vividness and the sheer quantity of detail. The anaphora and parallelism make us highly conscious of the item-by-item enumeration. After presenting the signs of death objectively as it were, the poet shifts to a commentary upon the scene (what C. Day Lewis calls "passionate statement"): [11] "al to late, al to late / wanne þe bere ys ate gate," and this shift is heightened by a doubling of the number of stresses within the line. The plan of the first section (lines 1–14) reappears in the second (lines 15–22), but with variations.* The repetition of the

---

* Section 1 has a series consisting of twelve two-stress lines; section 2 halves the series to six two-stress lines. In section 1, lines

basic line in the first section creates a sense of inevitability since we expect the repetition; the repetition of
the basic line in the second section creates a sense of in-
difference and thus prepares for the brilliant insouciance
of the last two lines. The inevitablity of death and the
consequent meaninglessness of worldly goods is scarcely
an original theme, but the sound structure of this lyric
so intensifies the moral lesson that it makes possible a
new contemplation of an old notion. The originality of
this lyric lies in its intensity. The second poem in this
same topic builds a more complicated sound structure,
one which we might call polyphonic:

When þi hed whaketh /
    memento;
When þi lippys blaken /
    confessio;
When thy brest pantis /
    contricio;
4   When þi wynde wantes /
    satisfactio;
When þi lymmes falys þe /
    libera me, domine;
When þi nase kelys þen /   *becomes cold*
    miserere;
When þine een holoen /
    nosce teipsum;
8   ffor then the deth ffolowes /
    Veni ad iudicium.[12]

In the first half of the sound structure (lines 1–4) the
Latin phrases harmonize with the English: both sections
of the line contain two stresses and either assonance or

1–2 and 11–12 use the same assonance, which unifies the section;
section 2 is unified by the recurrence in line 20 of the rime in line
15. The last two lines of section 2 return to the couplet form, metrically paralleling lines 13–14. This parallelism gives the poem a
sense of completion.

strong enough that we may argue for a measure of rest and the equivalent of three stresses in the second half. In the thought, each half of the line refers to the same event: the Incarnation (the east is traditionally associated with birth), the Crucifixion (west connotes death), the redemption (the south symbolizes Ecclesia), and the rejection of Christ (the north symbolizes Synagoga).[15] The second stanza now counterpoints the first. The line unit of the second stanza expands that of the first, yet retains enough verbal echoes from the first to point up a degree of similarity. Although each line can be read as containing six stresses, the number of unstressed syllables varies from line to line. Such a reading forces us to apply a principle which manifests itself in psalmody, where a prescribed formula takes precedence over the tonic accent of the words. The thought of the second stanza also counterpoints the first; the images here, as in the first stanza, refer to the Incarnation (as wedlock, in keeping with accepted glosses on several biblical passages, especially Ps. xviii. 6), the Crucifixion (as a joust, a very popular image), the redemption (as a purchasing, punning on the Latin *redimere,* to buy back), and Christ's rejection (as a pilgrim in a strange land). This counterpointing between stanzas points up an important unity; the shift in tenses (past to present grammatically, past to future notionally) and the shift in speaker indicate that the poem speaks of the two comings of Christ—the first at His Incarnation, the other on the Last Day. The poet uses his sound pattern and his parallel structure to fortify the analogy he sees in these two events. The portrayal of the Last Judgment in the second stanza does not emphasize the justice of God, but rather His mercy, goodness, and love; the images thus reveal more directly the same qualities which the first section implies. Moreover, if we recognize that God is merciful, good, and loving, we can appreciate the poignancy of the final line. But there is simultaneously a muted consciousness, from the reference to His acceptance and rejection, of Christ's role as judge and of the corresponding fact that men will receive their appropriate reward or punishment. The image of the north suggests His rejection by the Jews, which in turn is analogous to His rejection by all who choose to follow the devil rather than Christ. The poignancy of the rejection is increased by the image of the seeking Christ come all the way from heaven—a place some men will never know, and the search will have been all in vain. The image of the pilgrim connects to that of the north; according to a gloss on Job xix.15, Christ is a pilgrim because the Jews treated Him coldly.[16] These connotations enforce the analogy by which the Jews typify all who reject Christ. And the entire complex of relationships in the thought pattern is heightened by the corresponding complexities of the linear structure.

The second sound structure, monostrophic structure, uses the entire stanza, rather than the individual line, as its basic unit. The structure itself is merely one in which the same stanza form recurs throughout the song. The limitations of monostrophic structure come into sharpest focus when the poet has to fit his words to an already existing melody. He may have to juggle the tonic accents to accommodate the melodic stress. He may have to strain the syntax for the same reason, or restrict the possibilities of variety in phrasing to fit the rhythm. He may even be tempted to yield to his audience's delight in the melody by tacking on stanzas which do little or nothing to advance the thought. In short, he may sell out his poetry to pay for his music. A skilful poet can, of course, surmount these limitations, but the temptation to let the diction succumb to the music or rhythm is great.

If the poet relies on actual music to create the emotive structure, or if he relies heavily on his sound to approximate the hypnotic effect of the charm, he cannot permit himself a sharp change in mood; the same basic sound must serve two emotions.[17] He can, of course, intensify his emotion much more easily than shift it. If he allows himself the irregularity of the dramatic lyric, then obviously he can alter his sound for whatever purposes he sees fit. The song, however, is flexible enough to permit some change; not many of the religious lyrics exemplify a marked change, but "Nv yh she blostme sprynge" (XIII, No. 63) illustrates the kind of shift which is possible. The poem opens joyfully, and the rapid movement supports the tone of gladness:

	Nv yh she blostme sprynge,	*Now I see blossoms*
	hic herde a fuheles song.	*I heard bird's*
	a swete longinge	
4	myn herte þureþhut sprong	*throughout*
	þat is of luue newe,	
	þat is so swete and trewe	
	hyt gladiet al my song.	
8	hic wot mid ywisse	*know with certainty*
	my lyf and heke my blysse	*also*
	is al þar-hon ylong.	*thereon dependent*

The love turns out to be directed towards Jesus, but when the speaker examines this love, his tone changes to grief. His grief, however, is twofold: he commiserates with the suffering that Jesus underwent for his sins, and he recognizes simultaneously his own unworthiness and, worse, his spiritual lethargy:

	Away! þat hy ne can	
32	to hym tvrne al my þovt	*thought*
	and makien hym my lefman	*sweetheart*
	þat þvs me haued hy-bovt—	*has purchased*
	wyt pine and sorewhe longe,	*pain sorrow*
36	wyt wnde depe and stronge—	*wounds*
	of luue ne can hy novt.	
	hys blod fel to þe grvnde	
	hut of ys swete wnde	*out wounds*
40	þat of pyne hvs hauet hy-brovt.	*from torment*

The only concession the poet makes to slowing his meter occurs in the pause after *Away!* (line 31); the rapid movement, however, enforces the sense of helplessness which the speaker reveals in his inability to make Jesus his leman. This sense is then balanced by the lines which refer to all Christ has done for the speaker, and the rapid movement in this section suggests fragments of a possible long item-by-item enumeration. The meter moves too quickly for intense grief, but this grief is, in the context of the first two stanzas, assuaged by the joy which the speaker receives in contemplating the effects of Christ's suffering. Although the poet thus modifies the sorrow of his speaker, he at least makes an effort to depict the emotion, instead of passing over it as an established fact. Within the narrow limits he has set for himself, he succeeds.

To evaluate a poet's use of this monostrophic structure, we will have to appreciate his handling of pattern and variation. Sometimes the variation occurs within the pattern itself, especially in patterns of rime and meter; sometimes the change occurs from stanza to stanza. One device which reveals the use of pattern and variation in its most obvious form is incremental repetition. That it is so immediately recognizable accounts for part of its appeal. In one carol (Greene, No. 25) the only line of the quatrain which changes appreciably is the last; the only other change is the rime word in the second line.

> The sunne of grace hym schynit
>> in
>> In on day quan it was   *on a*   *when*
>> mor[we],
> Quan our Lord God born was
> 4   Withoute wem or sorwe.   *blemish*
>
> The sunne of grace hym schynit
>> in

> On a day quan it was pryme,
> Quan our Lord God born was,
> 8   So wel he knew his tyme. . . .

Although no music has survived for this carol, its structure suggests that two singers might have alternated singing the stanzas; the thought in the first two stanzas practically repeats itself, as it does in the last two. The only other significant feature about this carol is the unusual rime scheme if we consider the burden as part of each stanza: a b c b c a, and the a lines repeat one another exactly. The recurrence of the c and a rimes binds the burden closely to the stanzas. We might also note that the system of pauses illustrates the usual monostrophic pattern at its most obvious: exactly the same pauses fall in exactly the same places. With this we can compare "Lullay, lullay, litel child" (Greene, No. 155), which skilfully varies this tendency towards perfect regularity. Most of the lines, however, are end-stopped; in the opening stanza the sense spills over from one line to the other, but the final *d* sound forces a slight pause:

> Lullay, lullay, litel child,
> Thou that were so sterne and wild
> Nou art become meke and mild
> 4   To sauen that was forlore.

In the last stanza the parallel structure insists upon end-stopped lines, so that line 27 tends to be read as end-stopped rather than run-on, as the sense demands:

> That peine vs make of senne fre;
> That peine vs bringge, Jesu, to the;
> That peine vs helpe ay to fle
> 28   The wikkede fendes lore.

A similar use of parallel structure underscores the medial caesura in line 18:

> Lullay, for wo, thou litel thing,
> 18   Thou litel barun, thou litel king.

The medial caesura is the most conspicuous device the poet uses to vary his general penchant for the single-line phrase; in stanza six, however, he employs other pauses within the line:

> For man, that thou hast ay loued so,
> 22   Yet saltu suffren peines mo,
> In heued, in feet, in hondis to. . . .

This effective shifting in locating the pause from stanza to stanza prevents the meter from running away with the poem, as it does in many carols.

Other criteria for evaluating the poet's achievement in monostrophic structure center, to a special degree, in such familiar devices as alliteration, consonance, assonance, rime scheme, and variation in the number of feet per line. The following stanza from "Somer is comen" (XIII, No. 54) demonstrates most of these devices, and typifies the poet's excellent handling of his sound:

> Ihesu is þe childes name,
> 32   king of al londe;
> of þe king he meden game   *they*
> & smiten him wit honde
> to fonden him; opon a tre   *tempt*
> 36   he ȝeuen him wundes to & þre
> mi[d] honden;
> of bitter drinck
> he senden him
> 40   a sonde.   *serving*

Particularly effective are the repetition of the short *i* sound in lines 31–34 and especially as a substitute for rime in lines 38–39, and the variation of the *ond, on,* and *und* sounds (including the unaccented verb endings in

-en) in lines 34–37 and especially the patterning in *senden*
and *sonde* (lines 39, 40). Moreover, the poet skilfully
manipulates his variation in the number of feet per line
—from four to one—and utilizes a fairly complex rime
scheme.* Although the stanza form is complex, we can
readily detect the pattern, as indeed we must if we are
to take proper pleasure in the sound. An involved rime
scheme characterizes a group of carols which have a refrain as well as a burden. Sometimes part of the rime
scheme in the stanza appears in the burden as well, and
the burden includes the refrain; at the other extreme,
the burden uses a different set of rimes and does not repeat the refrain. In between these extremes, the possibilities are legion.[18]

The most complicated of the structures, the polystrophic, may vary its line length from stanza to stanza
or from section to section, or it may vary only its rime
scheme or meter. For example, "I saw a fayr maydyn"
(Greene, No. 143) does not deviate from its pattern of
rimed couplets, but it does alter its meter. Although the
number of stresses changes from line to line, most of the
lines break into sections of two or three stresses with a
pause separating the sections; and the interplay of these
two- and three-stress phrases creates a particularly pleasurable effect. Moreover, the very last line returns after
considerable variation to the pattern of the first line, and
we feel a keen satisfaction in hearing the pattern once
more.** A second example of metrical change, "þe fader
of heuene" (XV, No. 84; Greene, No. 148A), displays
a different kind of complexity. Here the metrical varia-

---

* Its basic scheme is a b a b c c b d d b, but the d rimes vary;
assonance appears in lines 18–19 and 38–39, and no rime at all in
lines 28–29 and 48–49. Variations also appear in other rimes.

**

      /   /   /   /
  I saw a fayr maydyn   syttyn and synge;

    /   /   /   /
  Grawnt hem his blyssyng   that now makyn chere.

tions coincide with variations in parallel structure. On the basis of its parallelism, the poem may be divided into four sections: stanza one; * stanzas two and three; stanzas four through nine; stanzas ten and eleven. Metrically, the poem divides into the same four sections. Each stanza has three lines, the third of which is the refrain. The first section uses a four-stress line followed by a three-stress line; the second section uses two four-stress lines; the third, seven-stress; the fourth, four-stress. The fact that the second and fourth sections share the meter of the burden pulls the parts of the poem together and reinforces its structure. In neither of these poems, however, does the variety in metrical structure seem to complement the thought in any particular way; it seems, in short, to be an end rather than a means. A similar ornamental use of polystrophic structure adorns two poems which vary their stanza form. "Crist makiþ to man a fair present" (XIV, No. 90) exhibits a simpler variation: one six-line stanza is followed by two monoriming quatrains; this pattern is repeated, then varied to a six-line stanza followed by three monoriming quatrains. These six-line stanzas differ from one another in their rime scheme.†
"Haill! Glaid and glorius" (XV, No. 22) ‡ builds an extremely complex system of pattern and variation and variation of the variation. The first stanza establishes a pattern of a b a b b$_3$, which it repeats. The second stanza follows this pattern exactly. The third stanza uses four stresses to the a line instead of three, and employs internal rime, but it maintains the same rime scheme.

* Following Greene's numbering; Brown prints the burden as stanza one.

† Stanza one is monoriming; stanza four has the scheme a a b a a b (Brown prints the stanza as four lines with internal rime); stanza seven, a a a a b b.

‡ Brown prints this lyric in stanzas of five and four lines, with one stanza of seven lines. On the basis of the rime scheme I think the poem should be printed in stanzas of ten lines (1–50, 75–84) and eight lines (51–74), with a final stanza of nine lines.

The fourth stanza varies this variation by using a different rime scheme in its last five lines. Stanza five varies this variation in both number of stresses and rime scheme, and so on. The first variation (stanza three) reappears in the penultimate stanza, and the pattern established in the first stanza reappears in the last stanza.* In a third example of polystrophic structure, the variation is easier to see, and it bears some significance in characterizing the speaker. "Ar ne kuthe ich sorghe non" (XIII, No. 5) alters the number of lines from stanza to stanza, but plays upon a basic rime scheme of a a b c c b. Stanza three uses this scheme twice; stanza four triples the a and c rimes; stanza five quadruples them.[19] Such repetition with variation corresponds roughly to the thought pattern, where certain ideas are repeated and varied, indicating the wandering thoughts and emotional upset of the speaker, who has been unjustly cast into prison (lines 13–14, 24–26).†

Two final examples of polystrophic structure exhibit a closer relationship between sound and meaning. "A child is boren amonges man" (XIV, No. 88; Greene, No. 12) presents the Incarnation as a political marriage between Christ and the soul by which man is freed from the devil's power. The tone of joy which this image suggests is furthered by the rapid meter and the strong beat in the introductory quatrain and the two six-line stanzas

---

* Except for the final b rime, since the stanza has nine lines instead of ten. We may represent the pattern of the entire poem as A A A¹ A² A³ B C A⁴ A¹ A. This use of pattern and variation loosely complements a similar technique in the thought; the poem consists of a series of epithets which praise Mary, and of various petitions sprinkled here and there.

† The rhythm moves gently, the variations in line length do not come abruptly, the meter flows smoothly. The tone is, in effect, extremely genteel. Such a tone fits the gentleness of the speaker, who possesses the Christlike quality of begging forgiveness for his enemies (lines 21–26), even if the poet does translate the "icele gentil sire" of his French original as "the wykke men" (line 22).

which follow. But the poet uses another device to express joy: a kind of incremental repetition which binds the third stanza to the second suggests something of a dance step, of taking so many steps in one direction, then reversing the direction:

> Senful man, be bliþe and glad,
> for your mariage þy peys ys
> grad,   *proclaimed*
>   wan crist was boren;
> 8 com to crist, þy peis ys grad,
> for þe was hys blod ysched,
>   þat were for-loren.
>
> Senful man, be bliþe & bold,
> 12 for euene ys boþe boȝt & sold,   *heaven*
>   euereche fote;
> com to crist, þy peys ys told,
> for þe he ȝahf a hondre fo[l]d,   *gave*
> 16 hys lif to bote.

This paralleling of lines 5 and 11, 8 and 14 thus supports the suggestion of dance in the first line of the burden: "Honnd by honnd we schulle ous take." A more complex relation of sound to sense appears in "Heȝe louerd, þou here my bone" (XIV, No. 6; see appendix), which successfully repeats certain motifs to suggest the rambling thoughts of the old man who speaks throughout the poem. It increases this sense of repetitiousness by alternating a twelve-line stanza with a five-line stanza. Moreover, the latter stanza modifies the last six lines of the former, so that this adds further to the sense of senility. The last stanza repeats the five-line form of the one which precedes it and serves as a kind of coda, as the thought of the final stanza concludes the whole. But the repetitiousness in the sound pattern is not confined to the stanza form. Stanza-linking repeats words, alliteration repeats sounds, the rime scheme repeats its rime at frequent intervals. All these techniques combine with the speaker's characterization and the depiction of his circumstances to increase the poem's emotive value. Finally, the poet sets his sound pattern to work to divide the thought into sections. He ties his stanzas together with concatenation, but at five places in his poem he fails to use this device, and at these points we can make a division of the thought.

This examination of the structures which contribute to the songlike qualities of the religious lyrics—polystrophic, monostrophic, linear—suggests some general observations about the role of sound in the poems. On the simplest level, sound may merely ornament a generally accepted notion—what oft was thought but ne'er so pleasurably expressed. Such poems as "Ar ne kuthe ich sorghe non" and "Haill! Glaid and glorius" require a degree of sophistication in their audience, for their effect depends upon more or less subtle variations in sound. They tend to point self-consciously to their techniques, and are often characterized by excesses of one kind or another. The courtly poets in particular are guilty of this kind of poetry, and one of their favorite forms of excess is aureate diction. In one sense, the variations which these poems employ seem to be ends in themselves. Actually they are a little more complex than that. A medieval religious poet might have defended his use of sound as ornament on a number of grounds. He might have argued, for instance, as did the Cluniac school of church ornamentation, that his sublime subject matter required the most beautiful handling of which he was capable. He might even have followed the defense of Suger of Saint Denis, who felt that sensible beauty can, with the aid of God, all the more readily transport us anagogically to the pleasures of heavenly beauty.[20] Hence the lavish use of Latin phrases, aureate diction, alliteration, internal rime, biblical imagery. Or the religious poet might have declared, more simply, that versification, as music itself, is based on number, proportion,

and harmony—which in turn lead man's thoughts to
God, so that the contemplation of his skill could lead
ultimately to the same goal as the contemplation of his
subject matter: to an apprehension of the perfect order
which is God Himself.[21] For the medieval man a definite
correlation existed between a poet's numbers and the
wisdom of his subject matter—a correlation which few
modern critics would be willing to accept. We content
ourselves instead with admiring the sound itself, not the
principle which it illustrates. On another level, the sound
may verify emotionally a valuable religious concept and
thus increase the emotional intensity of the audience's
belief. The medieval lyric poet is not so much interested
in making his audience understand the truths more
clearly as he is in enhancing its acceptance of them.[22]
Poems which ring with the sound of authority may enable
the simple hearer to accept mysteries which he is unable
to grasp intellectually, to accept them by accepting their
formulation. In "A child is boren amonges man," for
instance, the following lines speak of the Incarnation
and its effects:

> þat child ys god, þat child is man,
> 4   & in þat child oure lif bygan.

The pleasurable formulation of the mystery reaffirms
what the medieval audience must have heard before, but
the formulation is such that it obliges one to accept more
readily both the formulation and the mystery without
necessarily understanding the bases of either.* The songs
which pursue this goal are generally far less sophisticated

---

* The charm of these lines comes from the use of repetition
with variation. The balance in the two halves of line 3 varies in
the final word of each clause; the repetition of *child* in line 4 ties
the two lines together loosely. Since line 3 uses only three stressed
vowel sounds, the repetition of the *i* sound in line 4 in *in* and
child leads us to anticipate the recurrence of one of the other two
vowels of line 3. The word *lif* leads us to a greater anticipation;
when we hear the *a* sound from line 3 repeated in *bygan*, we are
satisfied.

than the lyrics whose sound ornaments the thought, but they possess a strong rhythm which tends to hypnotize. Finally, the sound in a lyric may have a third purpose: to assist in illuminating the subject matter. In the poems we have examined, this third purpose is seen most clearly in the lyrics on the signs of death and "Loue me brouhte." On the other hand, the poet may rely almost exclusively on his sound to establish the emotional intensity of the poem as a whole, as in "The fyrst day wan Crist was borne." A song may be loose in its thought structure, even inconsistent or incoherent, but if it achieves a charmlike effect, it has fulfilled its nature as song. If it ignores its thought, or its lyric situation, it limits its aesthetic achievement, but it is entitled to critical evaluation on the basis of what it does achieve. Religious song tends to be less complex than the dramatic lyric in its blending of sound, diction, lyric situation, and religious experience. But it has its own sphere: the handling of sound. In this sphere, the poets of the medieval religous lyrics at their best are outsung by only a small chorus of the best lyric poets in the language.

1. *Anatomy of Criticism* (Princeton, 1957), p. 256; "Lexis and Melos," *Sound and Poetry,* ed. Northrop Frye, English Institute Essays, 1956 (New York, 1957), p. xi. The quotation following is from *Anatomy,* p. 278.

2. *The Physical Basis of Rime* (Stanford, 1931), pp. 34, 41.

3. *Revelations of Divine Love,* ed. Grace Warrack (13th ed.; London, 1949), p. 51. Cf. with the tone of our poem: "And these be the works of Christ's Manhood wherein He rejoiceth; and that shewed He in the Ninth Revelation, where He saith: *It is a joy and bliss and endless pleasing to Me that ever I suffered Passion for thee"* (p. 63).

4. Sometimes these lines are printed "As clerkis fyndyn wretyn / in here book," as in E. K. Chambers, *English Literature at the Close of the Middle Ages,* Oxford History of English Literature, II² (New York, 1947), p. 91.

5. *Feeling and Form* (New York, 1953), p. 151. Cf. Lanz on the effect of rime, pp. 292–293: "For, being purely musical and depend-

ing entirely on sound, the effect is nevertheless very strong and often absorbingly intense. In view of this effect we often forget the emptiness of intellectual content and the vagueness of emotional associations. The beauty of the melody of vowels is forced into the center of attention. The logical sense retreats into the background."

6. *The Poetry of Experience* (London, 1957).

7. For a brief discussion of songbooks and minstrel collections, see Rossell Hope Robbins, ed., *Secular Lyrics of the XIVth and XVth Centuries* (2nd ed.; Oxford, 1955), pp. xxvi–xxviii. For facsimiles of some of the MSS with musical notation, see John Stainer, ed., *Early Bodleian Music* (London, 1901); for transcriptions of carols, see J. A. Stevens, ed., *The Mediaeval Carols,* Musica Britannica, IV (London, 1956).

8. See the discussion by Gustave Reese, *Music in the Middle Ages* (New York, 1940), pp. 172–174.

9. This poem seems to reflect something of the Bernardine concept of *memoria;* cf. Etienne Gilson, *La théologie mystique de Saint Bernard,* Études de Philosophie Médiévale, XX (Paris, 1934), p. 104: "La *memoria,* entendons par là la mémoire, le souvenir sensible de la passion du Christ, est en nous la condition et l'annonce de la *praesentia,* c'est à dire, au sens plein, de la vision béatifique dans la vie future, mais aussi déjà de ces visitations de l'âme par le Verbe en cette vie."

10. See Reese, p. 225.

11. *The Poetic Image* (London, 1947), p. 84.

12. Printed in Henry A. Person, *Cambridge Middle English Lyrics* (Seattle, 1953), p. 20, reprinted by permission of the University of Washington Press.

13. Printed in *English Fragments from Latin Medieval Service-Books,* ed. Henry Littlehales, EETS ES, XC (London, 1903), p. 8.

14. Cf. "In a Pistel þat poul wrouȝt" (XIV, No. 100), which discourses upon the same idea, taken here from I Thess. iv.4. For the conception of the motto as the "Tripos Apollinis," and the belief that it was stolen from the Song of Songs (i.7), see Henri de Lubac, *Exégèse médiévale* (Paris, 1959), I, 79, 157.

15. See, e.g., St. Gregory the Great, Homily I in Ezechiel, *PL,* LXXVI, 940. See also Emile Mâle, *The Gothic Image,* trans. Dora Nussey (New York, 1958), pp. 5–6; Louis Réau, *Iconographie de l'art chrétien* (Paris, 1955), I, 70–71.

16. *Allegoriae in Sacram Scripturam, PL,* CXII, 1027; *Glossa Ordinaria, PL,* CXIII, 809. See also Juliana of Norwich, p. 195; pseudo-Bonaventure, *The Mirrour of the Blessed Lyf of Jesu Christ,* trans. Nicholas Love (London, 1908), p. 86.

17. Sometimes the troubadour composers had difficulty with

changes of mood but simply ignored the change; see Théodore Gérold, *La musique au moyen âge* (Paris, 1932), pp. 165–168.

18. This same situation applies to the music of the carols and of the *chansons à refrain;* see Stevens, *passim,* and Gérold, pp. 128–129. Most of the fine points of variation undoubtedly got lost when the carols were set to music.

19. The music of this song bears the vaguest of resemblances to what goes on in the rime scheme. The melody of the first stanza is reasonably close—a a b a a b; the third stanza repeats and varies the a phrase throughout. The music is transcribed by Friedrich Gennrich, "Internationale mittelalterliche Melodien," *Zeits. für Musikwissenschaft,* XI (1928–29), 346–347.

20. See Edgar de Bruyne, *Études d'esthétique médiévale* (Brugge, 1946), II, 142–143.

21. This view is widespread from St. Augustine down; see *ibid.,* I, 332.

22. Cf. Louise Allen Armstrong, "The Mediaeval Latin Hymn," unpublished dissertation (The Johns Hopkins University, 1951), who speaks of the technique of St. Ambrose: "Association of concept is expressed by association of sound . . . the phrases themselves are so strikingly constructed that the device of iteration is sufficient to entrance the hearer into a state of affirmation even of mysteries beyond his grasp" (p. 33). As with Ambrose's lyrics, the Middle English lyrics were, in Mrs. Armstrong's words, "designed to play upon the periphery of the understanding, and aimed directly at emotional response" (p. 75).

CHAPTER TWO

THE LYRIC SITUATION

As well as differing in their handling of the sound, the song and the dramatic lyric differ in their treatment of the lyric situation.[1] In the song, the speaker is not sharply characterized; he tends to be anonymous, or Everyman. In the dramatic lyric, the speaker is sharply characterized because, among other things, the experience of which he speaks is so intense that he unconsciously (or consciously, for that matter) betrays a considerable part of his personality in presenting the experience. Moreover, the speaker in the song removes himself from his experience to sing of it rather than to dramatize it. His song presupposes that the events and people of which it sings contain values within themselves that the speaker merely reports. On the other hand, the dramatic lyric attributes a value to the people and events simply or primarily because they approximate actual experience. Reality in this type of lyric obviously centers around the self, and this emphasis upon the self is more typical of modern than of medieval times. A singer assumes that his audience shares in the values underlying his reported experience; he reports it, in fact, in terms

which reinforce the generally accepted and understood
forms of the emotion. When he offers a prayer to Christ,
he is, in a sense, speaking for all mankind and not just
for himself; he often interchanges *I* and *we* indiscrimi-
nately in the course of his song. But the speaker of the
dramatic lyric dramatizes an experience which has valid-
ity because it is his, because it imitates a particularized
reality. At one extreme of the dramatic lyric, the speaker
seems almost to insist that only he out of all mankind
has been subjected to the experience he dramatizes. Thus
the reader can share the experience vicariously through
the poem itself; he shares in the song, however, by bringing to it certain values which he holds in common with
the singer.

To indicate the degree to which the dramatic lyric
may be found in Middle English, we shall examine a
translation of a passage in St. Augustine's *Confessions*
and compare it with the original. The translation (XIV,
No. 5) reads as follows:

> Louerd, þu clepedest me *called*
> an ich nagt ne ansuarede þe *nought answered*
> Bute wordes scloe and sclepie: *slow sleepy*
> 4 "þole yet! þole a litel!" *wait*
> Bute "yiet" and "yiet" was
> endelis,
> and "þole a litel" a long wey is.

Since the material of the poem has been removed from
its total context, we shall identify the speaker merely as
a sinner, rather than Augustine, who has been called
personally by the Lord Himself. In any religious context
this personal calling should stimulate immediate action,
but the speaker's only answer is sleepy, indicating his
spiritual lethargy. But the speaker realizes both what he
should do and what he is doing; caught between his obligation and his lethargy in this most urgent of situations,
he is almost helpless. The fact that he can see precisely

his spiritual condition heightens the emotion of the entire poem, especially of the last two lines and of the note of sadness which the sound creates in them. That he directly addresses his Lord rather than himself fortifies his awareness of wanting to act and knowing he should. At the same time, the chosen address implies perhaps that the speaker would like the Lord to intervene once again and end his helplessness for him. In this context, the word *pole* (line 4) has an ambiguity which intensifies the speaker's characterization; the line has something of the effect of *"Permit* me to stay away from You just a little while longer." It is the tone of the child begging to be allowed to remain outdoors after the street lights are on. Perhaps there is also a reminder in *pole* of the crucified Christ, suffering for man's sins; the speaker thus asks Christ to endure this suffering just a bit longer until he can summon up enough strength of character to act. This last connotation places the speaker's answer in even sharper perspective in its recognition of the goodness of God and the purpose of His entire life on earth. It makes his answer all the more rank. Obviously, the speaker is not merely reporting his feelings, for reporting requires a certain aloofness, but he is caught up in his experience and dramatizes it as though it is actually happening at this moment.

The translation thus deserves the praise for its portrayal of human experience which George Kane has bestowed on it (p. 114). But then, curiously enough, he reverses its relationship to the original when he declares happily that the poet has made "the abstract expression of the original concrete." On the contrary, the poet has made it less concrete. The original carries a still greater emotional impact because it places its diction in a larger context so that the experience becomes more personal. The characterization of the speaker is basically the same, but more intensely drawn. The original appears above the translation in the MS (XIV, p. 244):

Non erat quid responderem tibi ueritate conuictus
dicenti mihi. *Surge qui dormis & exurge a mortuis
& illuminabit tibi* [sic] *Christus* [Eph. v. 14]. nisi
uerba lenta & sompnolenta. modo ecce modo. sine
paululum. sed modo & modo non habebant modum
& sine paululum in longum ibat.

First of all, Augustine is "ueritate conuictus," and this
conviction of the truth sharpens his spiritual struggle.
Moreover, in the lines preceding this passage, Augustine
equates the call with love of God, and his drowsiness
with his own cupidity. This also sharpens the struggle,
for Augustine realizes only too acutely just what spiritual
issues are at combat. Finally, the images of rising from
the dead and being illuminated echo other passages in
the work as a whole. In the first place, they emphasize
the necessity for action, but Augustine insists upon rising
to God from the death of the material world to the life
of the spiritual, and upon finding in God the goal of
his long search for wisdom. Thus, the image of illumina-
tion and light has many neo-Platonic connotations. When
we realize all these suggestions of the images, we see how
pressing the call becomes and how foolish Augustine
is in resisting. The passage in Augustine thus bears a
greater emotive content than our translation because
both the characterization of the speaker and the experience are more sharply drawn. I do not mean to disparage
the translator's achievement; I wish only to point out
how the vigor and complexity of the diction depend
partially upon the characterization of the speaker and
vice versa.

Symptomatic of the lack of this dramatic quality in
the medieval religious lyric is the absence of that most
personal of religious experiences, mysticism. Contrary
to the opinion of some commentators,[2] the number of
mystical lyrics is minute. Lowrey Nelson has offered a
commendable working definition of mystical poetry as

that which "concerns union in some way with the single
and transcendent supernatural," [3] and the few lyrics
which satisfy this definition barely flicker when compared to the flaming intensity of the lyrics of St. John
of the Cross, the "terrible sonnets" of Hopkins, or, for
that matter, the prose accounts of the medieval mystics.
If we compare the English version—it is not a translation
—of the great mystical hymn "Iesu Dulcis Memoria"
with its Latin original, we can detect a quality which
typifies the general vernacular handling of the mystical
experience.[4] The original describes the presence of God
in the soul with such intensity and sense of immediacy
that it must modify, even contradict one image with
another:

O beatum incendium, O ardens desiderium,
O dulce refrigerium, Amare Dei Filium. . . .
Iesu, sole serenior Et balsamo suauior,
Omni dulcore dulcior, Prae cunctis amabilior . . .
(O blessed glow, O burning desire, O sweet coolness,
to love the son of God. . . . Jesus, brighter than the
sun and more delightful than balsam, sweeter than
every sweetness, more lovable than all other things).

The English version describes the same phenomenon
less intensely:

Iesu, þou art so god a mon,
þi loue y ȝyrne al so y con;   *I desire*
þare fore ne lette me nomon,   *hinder*
148   þah ich for loue be blac ant   *pale and*
          won. . . .   *wan*

þi loue me makeþ so swyþe
    wod,
152   þat y ne drede for no flod.

Iesu, þi loue is suete & strong,
my lif is al on þe ylong!

The English poet has chosen a less fervid experience to sing of; he seeks to intensify it with his monostrophic repetition of rime and sentiment, but the analysis of the spiritual state is much less acute than in the Latin. The successful quest for Jesus in the original becomes a request in the vernacular, not for the union of the spiritual marriage on earth, but for final union in heaven. Nor does the poet realize the potentialities of his sound structure, as his Latin counterpart does, so that his poem fails as both dramatized experience and as song.

If the speaker-singer is characterized with less intensity than the speaker in the dramatic lyric, he often exhibits some individualizing traits which help create an impression of reality. But the poet is limited in his presentation of experience by convention; as Wright points out, what the speaker says "conform[s] largely to the audience's expectations derived from experience of other singers; through song the singer confirms and deepens the audience's conceptions" (p. 30). To accept such conventions is, of course, to limit the possibilities for individualizing the speaker's character. Such conventions, moreover, sometimes express themselves in actual formulas, as in some of the lyrics whose poets assume the persona of a sinner. At times the authors merely repeat the formulas without individualizing the speaker, indeed, without deepening the audience's conceptions; the poet relies on his audience to bring a ready-to-mix emotion to the poem. For instance, "The ten comawnde-mentis I haue broke" (XV, No. 138) sets down the commandments one by one, all of which the sinner has broken, and concludes perfunctorily with the speaker's decision to betake himself to God's mercy. The medieval audience may have been more willing to see itself in the speaker than is a modern audience, but the poem merely confirms the fact that the speaker is a sinner; it does not in any way enhance an understanding of sin. It depends for whatever effectiveness it has merely on the fact that

it does express a formula. In another, similar poem, the
speaker establishes himself as an evildoer by referring
to the formula incorporated into the *Confiteor* of the
Mass of having sinned "in thought, word, and deed"
(XIII, No. 65):

	for mi sinnis dred ham hi	*I am afraid*
	wen hi þenke þat hi sal bi	*I shall pay for*
8	þat hi haf mis hi-don	*what I have misdone*
	in worde, in worke, in þoith	*thought*
	foli.	*foolish*

Having thus established himself as a sinner, the speaker
proceeds to request Mary's aid. Another sinful fellow
elaborates upon the same formula (XIV, No. 124):

8	lord, haue mercy up-on my synne	
	þat i haue don seth y was born;	*since*
	wit word, wit wylle, wit herte, y-thouȝt;	*thought*
	wit flesch, wit blod, wit handes, wrouth;	
12	wit mouþ spoken, & be-for sworn.	

Later the speaker accuses himself of having committed
the "sinnes seuene" and of having broken the ten commandments (lines 19, 21), thus extending the formula
for the confession of guilt to include part of the approved
formula for the general confession of sin, which goes
roughly: I acknowledge myself guilty of the seven deadly
sins, of breaking the ten commandments, of not per-
forming the seven spiritual and the seven corporal works
of mercy, and of improper use of my five wits.[5] By referring to this formula, the speaker emphasizes his guilt for
the medieval audience. But the poetry of mere formula
is dreary stuff.

That such formulas can be handled effectively is demonstrated by "Leuedi sainte marie, moder and meide" (XIII, No. 2). Here the speaker fears greatly, for he has led a useless life all too long, and the poem develops this sense of helplessness and fear. He accuses himself of sinning in word and deed (line 21), omitting thought, and later repeats the accusation (line 29). He then singles out two of the deadly sins (lechery and gluttony, lines 22–23), and charges himself with failing to perform two corporal works of mercy (feeding the hungry and clothing the naked, line 26) and one spiritual (counseling the redeless, line 27). The poet thus suggests the form of the general confession—and consequently his speaker's utter sinfulness—without listing each item, and his choice of specific items heightens the illusion of reality. Other details add to this illusion; for example, the speaker mentions that his brown hair has now turned to white— he can't tell from what cosmetic—and his strong countenance has changed its hue (lines 19–20). These images create a sense of a wasted life, and a corresponding sense of helplessness. The last stanza strikes a particularly fine psychological note. The poem should end at line 40; the speaker has admitted his sinfulness, and the poem ends as it began, with an appeal to Mary. The last stanza, however, insists on the speaker's helplessness; he repeats his sinfulness, the fact that he had not heeded what men said to him of God, and his fear of judgment. Although the stanza is logically a kind of anticlimax, it actually climaxes the speaker's emotional state, for he cannot get out of his mind either his sinfulness or his fear that he has too little time left for atonement. This is a poem in which sin has a local habitation and a name.

When the medieval poets assume the identity of a sinner, they sometimes achieve a kind of intensity through their choice of addressee. As we might guess, the sinner-speaker usually prays to Christ or Mary; occasionally he prays to one of the saints, sometimes to the Trinity, but seldom to either God the Father or God the Holy Ghost. On a few occasions he soliloquizes. His attitude towards Christ varies: at times he stands in great fear, at others he reassures himself that Jesus will listen to his prayer, for He died to save all sinners. Less often the relationship between speaker and addressee is much more intimate, whether revealed by a series of apostrophes to Jesus, or by use of the image of Jesus as the soul's lover. But the crucified Christ and the baby Jesus invite the greatest emotional response; the poets often capitalize upon this fact and sink to bathos. The sinner-speaker generally addresses Mary either with absolute confidence in her intercession or else with an awareness of the wide gulf between her sinlessness and his own guilt and inadequacy in addressing so exalted a lady. The latter attitude probably underlies the series of poems which consist almost solely of Marian epithets. Mary was, of course, the well of mercy, and sinners had recourse to her when they feared the justice of her Son: as one speaker confesses, "Ihesu, seinte marie sone, þu i-her þin moder bone! [prayer] / to þe ne dar i clepien [call] noht, to hire ich make min mone" (XIII, No. 55, lines 33–34). And in a number of lyrics, the address shifts: sometimes from the speaker himself to Christ or Mary, often from Mary to Christ or vice versa. "Seinte mari, moder milde" (XIII, No. 16) devotes the first two stanzas to Mary, the second two to Jesus, and the last two to Mary again. This is not an unusual pattern. Obviously the sinner wants to take no chances about getting into heaven. Such shifting in "Iesu Crist, heouene kyng" (XIV, No. 8) bothers Brook (p. 17). The first and third stanzas address Christ; the second, Mary; and the final one is soliloquy. The speaker is merely utilizing the familiar formula of "Ad Jesum per Mariam." I do not deny the poem's structural looseness, but its shifts in address are psychologically appropriate and establish the tone suitable to a sinner who has recently forsaken his sins. The medieval poet's choice of addressee, including the shift from one person to another, contributes to an understanding of the emotional state in which the poet delineates his speaker. Although the speaker of a song is generally not delineated with the individuality characteristic of the dramatic lyric, he may be bedecked with a certain intensity when seen in relation to those to whom he prays.

Medieval poets often assume the persona of Christ, with effects less than brilliant, for the figure of Christ rarely emerges from the Divine Dark. In most of these poems Christ appeals to sinful man from the cross, often with less pathos than whine. Sometimes He reveals a pitiable wistfulness; but the anguish, the terrible sense of loneliness and of bearing the weight of the sins of the world are all glossed over, if even suggested. Such drama goes beyond the potentialities of the song. This *topos* seems to invite comparison with the medieval drama, but the technique is generally more homiletic than dramatic. Some of the lyrics were undoubtedly written for sermon use, and would gain in impressiveness if restored to the context of the total sermon as preached in a church. The preacher, for example, could take advantage of the presence of the crucifix, as the following preacher seems to do:

> Sires, beholdeþ before you the figure of oure redemptour Ihesu Crist, as he hongeþ in þe crosse in þe same fourme þat he suffred deþ in and brouʒt mankynde fro the peynes of helle. Wherfore he cryeþ and seiþ to vs yche day in syche wordes:

> > "Lystne, man, lystne to me,
> > Byholde what I thole for the.   *suffer*
> > To the, man, well lowde I crye;
> > For thy loue þou seest I dye.
> > Byholde my body how I am
> >   swongyn;   *scourged*

The number 4 appears in the left margin beside the fourth line of the poem.

Se þe nayles howe I am þrouȝ
  stongyn.   *pierced*
My body withoute is betyn sore,
8 My peynes with-in ben wel more.
All this I haue tholyd for the,
As þou schalt at Domysday se." [6]

The poem here provides the transition device from the Crucifixion scene, which the preacher has just dwelt upon, to the Last Judgment. The last line is particularly effective in its change of tone from mercy and love to threatening suggestions of justice. (The sermon continues the thought of the last two lines with a discussion of the Last Judgment.) What Chaucer's Pardoner might have done with such a lyric! But the modern reader in his easy chair does not participate in the speaker, the place, and the occasion. He has no recourse but to evaluate the poem as a literary artifact, and as such, he can only regret it no longer shares its larger context. Sometimes the poets use the addressee effectively, as when Christ addresses sinful man as "Be-holdet, al mi felawes, / ȝef ani me lik is founde" (XIV, No. 74, lines 3–4). The word *felawes* crackles. Christ has become one of us. He invites us to contemplate what terrible consequences this sharing involves. The poet has chosen this one word to focus his audience's attention on a religious fact they had taken for granted. Sometimes an image suddenly makes the characterization of Christ sharply alive, as the following (XIV, No. 51, lines 9–11):

> Biheld mi side,
> mi wndes sprede so wide;
> Rest-les i ride.[7]

For one brief moment the sound and imagery illumine the character of the dying Jesus.

  Few poems portray Christ as vividly as the following (XV, No. 111):

> I Haue laborede sore and suf-
>   fered dey₃th,
> and now I Rest and draw my
>   breyght;   *breath*
> but I schall come and call Ryght
>   sone
> 4   heuene and erght and hell to
>   dome;   *judgment*
> and thane schall know both
>   devyll and mane
> What I was and what I ame.

So anthropomorphic a portrayal may be unchristian, as Kane comments (p. 149), but the almost menacing tone of the last four lines suggests the Old Testament God of vengeance. The physical terms which the poet employs in his characterization are appropriate to Christ's human nature, and on Doomsday He will appear, according to medieval belief, with the signs of His Passion. The opening lines thus contrast with the final couplet, where the suggestion to the Hebrew formula of the divinity recalls Christ's own words, "Before Abraham was made, I am" (John viii. 58). Only at the Last Judgment the divine nature of the man-God will be made manifest, just as the poem itself comes to a full realization of the identity of Christ only in its conclusion. The concept of time which the poem reflects also establishes Christ's divinity. First, the time period between the Incarnation and Doomsday is limited to a period of rest, with connotations of brevity (and pure being) heightened by "Ryght sone" (line 3). Second, all time blurs in the final couplet into an eternal Now, when the future will establish for both devil and man what could only have been and must be simply because it is: Christ's divinity.

The medieval lyrists liked also to assume the persona of the Virgin Mary, and the Marian lament corresponds to Christ's complaints in popularity, technique, and ultimate aesthetic effect. The laments are characterized by apostrophes, rhetorical questions, swoons, addresses to the Jews, to the cross, to sinful man, to St. John, to Christ Himself.[8] Such poems exemplify the Franciscan appeal to basic emotions. Just as the affective school of piety utilized devices of sound to arouse the desired emotional response, so also it seized upon situations which inherently elicit normal human reactions, situations involving Mary or Mary and Christ. A mother lulling her infant son, a mother seeing her only son unjustly put to death, a lover who has given his very life for a beloved who was instrumental in his death—these are sure-fire situations because they appeal to some of our deepest emotions. Particularly in characterizing Mary, the Franciscan school exploits every aspect of the Mother-Son relationship. If the characterizations of the speakers are not subtle, they are intense, and the addressees heavily reinforce the emotion of the speaker. Notice, for example, the effectiveness of this stanza from a Marian lament (XV, No. 7):

> O woman, woman, wel is the,
> Thy childis cap þu dose vpon;   *put on*
> þu pykys his here, be-holdys   *comb*   *behold*
>   his ble,   *color*
> 12 þu wost not wele when þu hast *know not*
>   done.   *happiness*
> But euer, alas! I make my mone
> To se my sonnys hed as hit is
>   here;
> I pyke owt thornys be on & on,   *one by one*
> 16 ffor now liggus ded my dere son   *lies*
>   dere.

These lines gain an intensity because they are spoken by Mary to all mothers; they capitalize upon human maternal instincts and transfer this emotional response to another plane. Within this context, the striking pun on *pykys* and *pyke* (lines 11, 15) gains further effectiveness. But the emotion is not very complex to begin with, and it is diluted over eighty-eight lines. We find this same basic sort of appeal when Mary addresses her infant Son (XIV, No. 75):

> Ihesu, suete sone dere,
> 8   In porful bed þu list nou here,   *poor*
>   & þat me greuet sore;
>   For þi credel is als a bere,   *as a bier*
>   Ox & Asse ben þi fere—   *companions*
> 12   Wepen may I þer fore.
>
> Ihesu, suete, be nout wroth,
>   I haue neiþer clut ne cloth   *rag*
>   þe inne for to folde;
> 16   I ne haue but a clut of a lappe;
>   þerfore ley þi feet to my pappe,
>   & kep þe fro þe colde.
>
>   Cold þe taket, i may wel se.
> 20   For loue of man it mot be
>   þe to suffren wo,
>   For bet it is þu suffre þis
>   þan man for-bere heuene blis;
> 24   þu most him biȝen þer-to.   *redeem*

The diction works very well within this specific context; Mary undoubtedly is thinking of the barrenness and poverty of the cradle when she thinks of it as a bier (line 10), but we think, of course, of the paradox that Christ was born to die, and the cradle becomes the cross. The poet also juxtaposes the shivering Baby and the bleeding Man, thus forming a composite suffering Christ (lines 20–21). The isolation of Christ from the rest of men so that His only playmates are an ox and an ass (line 11) reminds us of the loneliness of the Crucifixion. And when we read the line in view of the alternative in lines 22–23, we realize even more forcibly that man should be Christ's fere. These connotations prepare for the emotive climax (line 24), when Mary imparts a sense of obligation to Christ as Savior. The effect underscores the notion of the intense suffering which man has forced Christ to endure for him. And above all, the emotion is accentuated by being spoken by a mother to her newly born, shivering Baby. Franciscan poetry in general recognizes what the speaker, the addressee, and the general context can do for a poem's emotive value. The technique is limited; we can quickly read our fill. But the effect is there.

The most interesting of the Marian characterizations, "That lovely lady sat and song" (Greene, No. 150B), also works within the Franciscan tradition. What we have in the Bodleian version of this lullaby carol is a miniature portrait of Mary as help of sinners. Her technique in interceding for mankind reminds us of her behavior in the miracles of the Virgin; in the carol, however, she is much more subtle, for she is not so much Queen of Heaven, as in the miracles, as she is Mother of Christ. Twice Mary asks her Son why, since He is king of heaven and earth, He lies in such poverty, but He never explicitly answers; He simply assures her that He has as witnesses to His kingship the angels, representative of His heavenly kingdom (stanza two), and lords, dukes, and kings—in particular the Magi—all representatives of His earthly kingdom (stanza four). Twice He assures Mary that He has willed His poverty, and she accepts this as the answer to her question *why*. She then moves one step further in her approach to her Son; she wants to know how she can make Him "glad of chere," adding: "For al thi wyll / I wold fullfyll" (lines 44–46). He answers by requesting to be treated as any baby: to be set on her knee, warmed in her arms, sung to when He cries. This request that Mary fulfill her role as mother plays into Mary's hands. Her Son has made three requests of her for lulling; now she makes a request of Him:

that God created man to be mindful of former mirths and thereby to come to Him, or relatedly, that God created man for happiness with Him in heaven. The line thus glances back at the joys of the old man's past life and anticipates the joys of his future life in heaven. The motif appears in lines 12, 13, 43, 65, 80, and 81 and generally underscores the contrast between old age and youth. It culminates in "Murþes helpeþ me no more" (line 92), part of the sinner's renunciation of all earthly joys and preparation for his complete renunciation of self. But in addition to presenting these general qualities of old age, the poet also individualizes his speaker. At one time, says the old man, the ladies were glad enough to have him in their bowers, but now he "may no fynger folde," he is little loved and even less regarded (lines 18–23); he is plagued by gout and many other evils (lines 24–25); although he once cut a fine figure on a horse and dressed himself in expensive clothing, now all his property is gone, and his only steed is his cane (lines 30–34); while he sees the horses strong in their stalls, he goes limping, and his heart sinks (lines 35–37).

When he characterizes the old man as a sinner, the poet also approaches the technique of the dramatic lyric. The experience which the speaker undergoes is more intense than we usually encounter, but the poet has not used his verse as freely as he should have to achieve maximum intensity. The old man reviews his past life twice, the second time with a greater consciousness of his guilt. He accuses himself of the seven deadly sins (substituting lying for anger) and personifies them to show how intimately he lived with them.[9] Although the acknowledgement of all seven follows the general formula for confession, it conforms also to the psychology of the penitent who feels most sharply the nature of God, of the creature-Creator relationship, and thus experiences an immediate sense of sin. But one line intrudes: "Monne mest y am to mene" (line 66); self-

pity deters his spiritual progress, for he must completely
renounce his selfhood. His consciousness of sin seems
to make him forget for a moment that he no longer can
be the sinful man he was, and he asks for the grace to
abandon his wild life (lines 67–68). He realizes the necessity of humility (line 71), but we wonder whether he
doesn't really look back on his early days with an in-
appropriate touch of nostalgia (lines 81–85). He is not
yet ready for forgiveness. Finally, however, he recognizes that he has been so beset with sorrow that he has
been brought to the ground (lines 95–97); only at this
point does he use the third person rather than the first.
Once he has forced himself to realize he is nothing—not
even *I*—he can identify the remedy for his sorrow which
he half perceived all along. Here the tone changes. The
old man now has attained a spirit of resignation, of
hopefulness; he perceives that he is ready for death. He
concludes with a prayer, not just for himself, but for
all men:

God vs lene of ys lyht	*grant*	*light*
þat we of sontes habben syht		*saints*
ant heuene to mede! Amen.		*as reward*

He has learned his lesson of Christian humility.

Several times in the poem the old man seems to
shift his addressee. He begins by addressing God, then
appears to be talking to himself, and then speaks to God
directly three more times (lines 50, 67, 70) before his
thoughts wander away again (especially in lines 75–77).
He addresses death with a cry of anguish (lines 86–88),
seems to speak to himself once more, and finally turns to
God (lines 105–107). This shifting from one addressee to
another and back again not only suggests senility, but
also complements the progression in the old man's spiritual state. His nostalgia and self-pity draw his attention
from his spiritual state, and only after his apostrophe to
death does he recognize he is not yet ready spiritually

for death. Thus the shifts enhance the emotional intensity with which the poet delineates his speaker.

Finally, within the context of the lyric situation, the diction acquires emotional vitality. Two epithets, *fulle-flet* [fill-floor] and *waynoun wayteglede* [good-for-nothing who sits-gazing-at-the-fire], carry strong emotional connotations and come early in the poem (lines 16, 17) so we can read the old man's memories with the proper awareness of his present state. In effect, the old man becomes all the more pathetic. The fine contrast between his early prowess as a horseman and his present dependence upon a cane, his only steed (lines 30, 34), receives even greater emotional stress from the context. The comparisons to the haughty servant and the head hound (lines 84–85) [10] have connotations not only of pride but of vigor and activity, and thus remind us strongly of the speaker's feebleness and inertia. Even the cliché "wild as a roe" (line 27) works well within the total context. The biblical image of the fading flower (Job xiv. 2; line 90), another cliché, here has the suggestion of a flower which someone has plucked and then tossed away when it began to fade, a suggestion which sums up the old man's condition, and incidentally prepares for the complete humility which he feels later (lines 96–97). Although clichés abound in songs, they can be vitalized by the context, as they are in this poem. As the poem also demonstrates, although the song has a different emotive structure from the dramatic lyric because of its handling of the lyric situation, it still enables the poet to manipulate his lyric situation so that his poem may give an emotional intensity to a generally accepted religious concept. The poet of the medieval religious lyric borrows from the religious tradition not only his subject matter but also the form into which he casts his materials. He may either assimilate this form into the lyric situation, where it gains vitality, or he may so loosely join the two that he does little to enhance the situation inherent in the form itself. But these are matters to be considered in Chapter Three.

1. For my comments on the dramatic lyric, I am indebted to J. Craig La Drière, "Voice and Address," *Dictionary of World Literature,* ed. Joseph T. Shipley (rev. ed.; New York, 1953), pp. 441–444; George T. Wright, *The Poet in the Poem* (Berkeley, 1960); C. M. Ing, "Lyric," *Cassell's Encyclopaedia of Literature,* ed. S. H. Steinberg (London, 1953), I, 354–355.

2. Especially Patterson, p. 4, and Rossell Hope Robbins, "Two Fourteenth-Century Mystical Poems," *MLR,* XXXV (1940), 320.

3. "The Rhetoric of Ineffability: toward a Definition of Mystical Poetry," *CL,* VIII (1956), 324.

4. The Latin texts have been edited by André Wilmart, *Le "Jubilus" de Saint Bernard,* Storia e Letteratura, II (Rome, 1944). For a discussion of the mystical elements, see Etienne Gilson, "Sur le *Iesu Dulcis Memoria,*" *Speculum,* III (1928), 322–334; "La mystique cistercienne et le Iesu dulcis memoria," in *Les idées et les lettres* (2nd ed.; Paris, 1955), pp. 39–57. The English version has been edited by Karl Böddeker, *Altenenglische Dichtungen des MS. Harl. 2253* (Berlin, 1878), pp. 198–205.

5. For poems based on this formula, see Carleton Brown and Rossell Hope Robbins, *The Index of Middle English Verse* (New York, 1943), Nos. 3231, 3233. One version of the latter appears in XIV, No. 87.

6. Printed in *Speculum Sacerdotale,* ed. Edward H. Weatherly, EETS, CC (London, 1936), p. 112.

7. Brown incorrectly glosses *ride* as "be suspended" (p. 341).

8. For the Marian lament, see George C. Taylor, "The English Planctus Mariae," *MP,* IV (1907), 605–637, esp. pp. 614–615.

9. I do not accept the suggestion of Morton Bloomfield, *The Seven Deadly Sins* (East Lansing, 1952), p. 154, that in this section the speaker is "conceived as a castle." The poet may have been influenced by a presentation of the sins as the devil's castle, but the image seems hardly applicable to our poem since castles do not ordinarily have bedfellows (line 62).

10. Brook, p. 81, glosses *heued-hount* as "chief huntsman," but "head hound" suggests to me more of a sense of pride, and I accept it as a better gloss.

CHAPTER THREE

SOME
RELIGIOUS STRUCTURES

The medieval poet's religion did more than furnish him with a subject; it placed at his disposal a number of forms into which his subject could be cast. He could not only sing of a topic whose value was taken for granted, but could also express it in a form whose value might be assumed. Forms with such built-in response were not just convenient; they could prove poetically dangerous. As we have seen in our discussion of the formula for the confession of sin, the poet sometimes relied exclusively upon the form and saved himself the task of specifying the speaker's guilt. If he made any pretense at analyzing his speaker's spiritual condition, the generality of the formula could easily lead to poetic disaster. But as we have also observed, some poets did cut the formula to the thought. In effect, to use Coleridge's well-known distinction, some poets handled the formula mechanically, others organically. Or as T. S. Eliot has described the difference, some poets

> have recourse to pouring their liquid sentiment into
> a ready-made mould in which they vainly hope that

it will set. In a perfect sonnet, what you admire is
not so much the author's skill in adapting himself
to the patterns as the skill and power with which
he makes the pattern comply with what he has to
say.[1]

By religious forms, however, I do not mean merely the
religious equivalent of a literary form like the sonnet;
I mean a generally accepted formulation of any phase
of the spiritual life which automatically enables the poet
to arrange his materials in some kind of sequence. For
example, the convention that when one prays, he should
pray not only for himself but for others. This convention
explains at least partially the sequence in two very
popular poems, "Ihesu lorde, þat madest me" (Richard
de Caistre's hymn; XV, No. 64) and "Marie moder, wel
the be" (XIV, No. 122).[2] Each part of the former poem
is concluded in the MS by the rubric "Pater noster. Aue
maria." The latter poem is more carefully unified. After
an introductory stanza, the speaker devotes five stanzas
in petition for himself, four stanzas in petition for others,
and two concluding stanzas for both others and himself.
By examining some of the forms which medieval religion
thus made available to the poet, and by determining
whether the poet has handled these forms mechanically
or organically, we can arrive at a fairer evaluation of
the literary quality of the Middle English religious lyric.

When we examine the accounts of the spiritual state
in the lyrics, we do not find much use of such over-all
patterns as the traditional threefold mystical way—the
purgative, the illuminative, and the unitive. I have already commented that the English poets wrote few gen-
uinely mystical poems; those they did compose, however,
tend to rely more on emotional fervor than strict stanzaic
sequence. Theoretically at least, such formlessness expresses the psychological condition of the speaker, and
the emotion in a very real sense shapes the poem. In

mystical poetry we have a further difficulty, for as Evelyn
Underhill comments, the mystic poet's audience "must
be bewitched as well as addressed, caught up to something
of his state, before they can be made to understand." [3]
Since the root of the mystical experience is in the love
the soul feels for God, perhaps we should not expect to
find too rigid a set of controls, for rigidity can militate
against emotion. But at the same time there can be
some basis for stanzaic progression. Let us examine two
poems which do employ some such basis. The first is
"Luf es lyf þat lastes ay" (XIV, No. 84); it belongs to the
school of Richard Rolle. The traditional threefold mystical way does not apply exactly to Rolle's experience;
moreover, he uses his own progression of *calor, canor,* and
dulcor, and it seems best to accept this progression as the
particular religious form we are examining. Few of
Rolle's poems utilize this progression to determine the
stanzaic sequence; this poem, however, does employ it,
but very loosely. After an introductory stanza, the speaker
mentions *calor* in line 6; he anticipates the advancement
to *canor* with a reference in line 24 to "þe sang of þi
louyng," but interrupts the progression with a discussion
of the mutability of earthly things. Finally he returns to
canor in line 67 and moves quickly to *dulcor* in line 73.
This section includes a brief consideration of Christ's
passion (lines 85–88), then returns to the motif of sweetness (line 89), and concludes with a petition to love Jesus
"withowten endyng" (line 96). This poem relies at least
partially upon its audience's familiarity with Rolle's
system in order to create its emotional impact. The
stanzas which speak of *canor* do seem more intense than
those which describe *calor,* but they also seem more
intense than the section on *dulcor.* The audience who
knows Rolle's terminology will bring that knowledge to
the poem and invest the final section with a greater
emotional intensity than the section warrants in itself.
Like most of Rolle's lyrics, this one rambles—but his

didactic purpose (line 4) has much to do with it. Poems such as this were meant to be savored; they were devotional stimuli. Their readers were undoubtedly familiar with the kind of advice St. Anselm prefaced to his meditations: to abandon the text and meditate as frequently as they saw fit, to use as much of the author's meditation as they found useful.[4] The formlessness of Rolle's lyric is thus formlessness with a purpose, but it is probably better evaluated as a poetic devotion than as a devotional poem.

The second lyric which is structured on a definite sequence in the spiritual life is "In a valey of þis restles mynde" ("Quia amore langueo").[5] It follows the state of man's soul from her baptism through her sinfulness to her conversion, through the Purgative Way of beginners to the Illuminative Way of the proficient. It stops short of the Unitive Way and concludes instead with a suggestion of final union with Christ in heaven. The poem teems with imagery in the mystical tradition; much of it comes from the Song of Songs. Kane has already noted the frequent shifts in the presentation of Christ:

> The knight wounded by love, the relentless hunter, the eager suitor, the bridegroom, the parent, the husband follow hard upon one another in the poet's fancy, and one concept slips into the next with an ease made possible only by the high excitement of his creative faculty (pp. 159–160).

Also making it possible is the mystical tradition and its tendency to modify one image by another. The poem opens with the speaker's search for true love in the mountains and meadows of his "restles mynde"; here he soon finds the object of his search, Christ Himself ("The kingdom of God is within you," Luke xvii.21—a favorite passage among the mystics). Christ then becomes the speaker and demonstrates the truth of his refrain, "Quia amore langueo." He longs for the soul of man, who has

abandoned Him (lines 22, 79). The poet then wittily
employs the familiar image of clothing in a section on
the Passion. Christ has clothed man's soul "in grace &
heuenli liȝt" (line 27)—i.e., the grace of baptism—while
she has placed upon Him "þis bloodi scherte" (line 28),
has embroidered His white gloves with blood (lines
42–44), and has buckled His feet "With scharp naile"
(lines 51–52)—i.e., she has caused the Crucifixion because
of her sinfulness. But Christ, in turn, will make His body
"hir hertis baite" (line 55). This emphasis upon Christ's
humanity and especially upon His Passion conforms to
the importance given it in mystical treatises as the richest
subject for meditation. This concept expands in the
next stanza to include one of the most important images
in the poem: the chamber in Christ's side wherein He
and man's soul will sleep together (lines 57–60). After
proving His eagerness to be united with man's soul,
Christ now formally invites her to come to Him:

> Fair loue, lete us go pleye!
>   Applis ben ripe in my gar-
>   dayne;
>   I schal þee cloþe in a newe aray,
> 84   Þi mete schal be mylk, hony,
>   & wiyn.
>   Fair loue, lete us go digne,   *dine*
>   Þi sustynaunce is in my
>   crippe, lo!   *scrip*
>   Tarie þou not, my fair spouse
>   myne,
> 88   Quia amore langueo.

The reference in line 81 may be to the "love game" of
coming and going which Christ plays in man's soul; [6]
it would thus anticipate the tribulation of line 123, that
feeling the soul experiences when deprived of the consolation of Christ's presence. The reference to Christ's
nourishing the soul foreshadows the image of the baby

(line 107). The soul now responds to the invitation; she has presumably done as Christ asked (stanza thirteen) and looked out of her bodily house through the windows of kindness—i.e., forsaken fleshly desires and abandoned the things of this world. This stage has been described in "Gold & al þis werdis wyn" ("I would be Clad in Christis Skin," XIV, No. 71), which contains some close parallels to this section of our poem.[7] The soul is now at last in her chamber (line 105), undoubtedly the chamber in Christ's side mentioned earlier.

This chamber in which the soul rests is not just the bridal chamber, but also, paradoxically, the nursery:

> My loue is in hir chaumbir:
>   holde ȝoure pees,
> Make ȝe no noise, but lete
>   hir slepe.
> My babe y wolde not were in
>   disese;   *discomfort*
> 108   I may not heere my dere
>   child wepe.
> With my pap y schal hir
>   kepe.

The food imagery of the earlier stanzas thus relates not just to the union of Christ and the soul, but also to the concept of Christ as Mother and the soul as child. The overtones of "Thy breasts are better than wine" (Songs i.1) enhance the poet's punning. The images in this section are paralleled in the writings of the mystics; Juliana of Norwich, for example, says in a similar passage: "The Mother may lay the child tenderly to her breast, but our tender Mother, Jesus, He may homely lead us into His blessed breast, by His sweet open side, and shew therein part of the Godhead and the joys of heaven."[8] Henry Suso also uses the image of the soul as baby to describe the Illuminative Way; then the Eternal Wisdom (Christ as Mother) tells him: "Thou hast been a child at the breast, a spoiled child. . . . Now I will withdraw all this." Similarly, John Tauler observes: "Think not that God will be always caressing His children, or shine upon their heads, or kindle their hearts, as He does at the first. . . . We . . . must now serve the Lord with strenuous industry and at our own costs." In our poem Christ also warns the soul that He will not always feed it with children's food (lines 117–118), but that the soul may expect to be tried and her love refined through adversity. "I wole preue þi loue wiþ aduersite" (line 119), says Christ, and the experience of the mystics confirms His promise. Such periods of adversity seem most characteristic of the Illuminative Way, once the soul is advanced on the route of perfection, and the description of the state of the soul in our poem corresponds to what the mystics write of it. The poem concludes with Christ's request that the soul, "Myn owne wijf" (line 126), not depart from Him, and with the promise that "þi meede is markid whan þou art mort [dead]" (line 127). The images, antitheses, paradoxes have tumbled one after another throughout this poem in an excited flurry—underscoring the love of the languishing Jesus. These devices point also to the soul's progress in yielding to Christ's love. The poet has thus organically used the accepted sequence in the biography of spiritual perfection in order to express his religious subject matter.

The loose thought pattern which characterizes many of these religious songs is not much tightened if a poet uses another form, borrowed from religious devotion— the liturgical formula of address plus petition. This formula, in fact, tends to irritate many modern readers, for the poem which utilizes it treads water for stanza after stanza, repeating and repeating and repeating the theme in all its ramifications. Not progression but sheer force of repetition gives such a poem structure. Many poems which use the technique address the Virgin Mary; they pile up a series of epithets introduced by anaphora (usually *hail*) and followed by a petition. Sometimes the petition concludes every stanza; sometimes it concludes only the final stanza; sometimes it crops up here and there throughout the poem. The anaphora may introduce every line, or merely every stanza. The form is certainly flexible enough; a good poet can make it buttress the emotive pattern. He generally gives himself the best chance of success if his poem is short, like "Swete ihesu, king of blisse" (XIII, No. 50). When he handles the formula badly, however, the emotional fervor evaporates long before the poet runs out of epithets. If a certain amount of repetition can create an emotional intensity, it does not follow that twice the amount of repetition will double the intensity. William Dunbar, for example, gives us too much of a good thing in his ballade in praise of Mary. He not only flogs his rimes, he pushes the address-plus-petition form further than the content can effectively support:

	Hale, sterne superne! Hale, in eterne,	*above*
	In Godis sicht to schyne!	
	Lucerne in derne for to discerne	*lamp* *darkness*
4	Be glory and grace devyne;	
	Hodiern, modern, sempitern,	
	Angelicall regyne!	
	Our tern inferne for to dispern	*trouble disperse*
8	Helpe, rialest rosyne!	
	Ave Maria, gracia plena!	
	Haile, fresche floure femynyne!	
	Yerne us, guberne, virgin matern,	*govern*
12	Of reuth baith rute and ryne.[9]	*root rind*

Dunbar varies the formula skilfully enough; his basic pattern is address, petition, address (line 1–6, 7–8, 8–9), which he repeats (lines 10, 11, 11–12). Such abundant address certainly gives the petition an emotional intensity, but the tone becomes almost nagging. The liturgical formula, as the rime, winks too self-consciously from the page.

The structure of address plus petition is applied most prominently in the Litany of the Saints, and a number of lyrics borrow this form. "Jhesus, for thi holy name" (Greene, No. 309) and "Mary, moder of mercy & pyte" (XV, No. 124) address various groups of saints in a succession of stanzas. Their obvious patterning upon the Litany lends an added solemnity and, from the frequent addresses, a sense of urgency. They follow generally the order of address in the Litany and retain or add an appropriate tag at the end of each stanza, but they lack the sectional divisions of the Litany and therefore are less complex than "Kyrieleyson, haue mercy, good lorde," [10] a prayer for England. The form is particularly appropriate since the Litany was recited on just such occasions as the poem indicates. The poem divides into as many sections as the Litany, each division marked by the appropriate changes in response. It even concludes with the Agnus Dei and the Kyrie. But using this form has drawbacks which the poets do not always overcome. Utilizing each address without adding the proper petition removes much of the hypnotic quality of the original—a loss the poets sometimes compensate for by using a refrain. A second drawback is that, with the musical value weakened, the inclusion of so many stanzas means that the sheer quantity of address may become wearisome. If, however, the hypnotic quality of the lyric successfully approximates that of the Litany, and if the petition strikes a note of urgency, the sound and the sense complement one another, and the tone pulls the parts together. Probably the most successful of the three lyrics is "Mary, moder of mercy & pyte," primarily because it has an effective sound pattern and because it is short.

That the formula of address plus petition can succeed in a longer poem is evidenced by the following lyric
attributed to William of Shoreham (XIV, No. 32):

	Marye, mayde mylde and fre,	*noble*
	Chambre of þe trynyte,	
	One wyle lest to me,	*a while*
4	Ase ich þe grete wyþ songe:	
	Þaȝ my fet on-clene be,	*vessel unclean*
	My mes þou onder-fonge.	*prepared food receive*
	Þou art quene of paradys,	
8	Of heuene, of erthe, of al	
	þat hys;	
	Þou bere þane kynge of blys	
	Wyþ-oute senne and sore;	
	Þou hast y-ryȝt þat was amys,	
12	Y-wonne þat was ylore.	*lost*
	Þou ert þe coluere of noe	*dove*
	Þat broute þe braunche of	
	olyue tre,	
	In tokne þat pays scholde be	
16	By-tuexte god and manne.	
	Suete leuedy, help þou me,	
	Wanne ich schal wende	
	hanne.	*hence*
	Þou art þe bosche of synay,	
20	Þou art þe rytte sarray,	*Sara*
	Þou hast ybrouȝt ous out of cry	
	Of calenge of þe fende.	*claim*
	Þou art crystes oȝene drury,	*sweetheart*
24	And of dauyes kende.	*tribe*
	Þou ert þe slinge, þy sone	
	þe ston,	

Þat dauy slange golye op-on;   *David   Goliath*
Þou ert þe ӡerd al of aaron   *you are the barren*
28   Me dreye iseӡ spryng-   *rod of Aaron which*
        ynde.   *people saw blossoming*
Wyt-nesse at ham euerechon   *every one*
Þat wyste of þyne chyldynge.   *knew*

Þou ert þe temple salomon,
32   In þe wondrede gedeon;   *marveled*
Þou hest ygladed symeon   *gladdened*
    Wyþ þyne swete offrynge
In þe temple atte auter-ston   *at the altar stone*
36   Wyþ ihesus heuene kynge.

Þou ert Iudith, þat fayre wyf,
Þou hast abated al þat stryf;
Olofernes wyþ hys knyf   *Of Holofernes*
40   Hys heuede þou hym by-
        nome.   *took away*
Þou hest ysaued here lef   *their life*
Þat to þe wylle come.

Þou ert hester, þat swete þynge,
44   And asseuer þe ryche kynge
Þe heþ ychose to hys weddynge   *Thee hath chosen*
    And quene he heþ a-uonge;   *taken*
For mardocheus, þy derlynge,
48   Syre aman was y-honge.

Þe prophete ezechyel
In hys boke hyt wytnesseþ wel,
Þou ert þe gate so stronge so
        stel
52   Ac euere y-schet fram manne;
Þou erte þe ryӡte uayre rachel,   *fair*
Fayrest of alle wymman.

By ryȝte toknynge þou ert þe
    hel   *hill*

56   Of wan spellede danyel;   *which*   *spoke*
    Þou ert emaus, þe ryche castel
    Þar resteþ alle werye;   *where*
    Ine þe restede emanuel

60   Of wan y-spekeþ ysaye.   *whom*

Ine þe hys god by-come a chyld,
Ine þe hys wreche by-come   *wrath*
    myld;
Þat vnicorn þat was so wyld

64   Aleyd hys of a   *is subdued by a chaste*
    cheaste: *woman*
Þou hast y-tamed and i-styld
Wyþ melke of þy breste.

Ine þe apocalyps sent Iohn

68   Iseȝ ane wymman wyþ sonne   *saw a*
    by-gon,
Þane mone al onder hyre   *the moon*
    ton,   *toes (feet)*
    I-crouned wyþ tuel sterre: *twelve stars*
    Swyl a leuedy nas neuere non   *such*   *was*

72   Wyþ þane fend to werre.   *fiend*   *war*

Ase þe sonne takeþ hyre pas   *way*
Wyþ-oute breche þorȝ-out þat *breach through-*
    glas,   *out*
Þy maydenhod on-wemmed hyt was *unblemished*

76   For bere of þyne chylde.   *bearing*
Nou, swete leuedy of solas,
    To ous senfolle be þou
        mylde!

Haue, leuedy, þys lytel songe

80   Þat out of senfol herte spronge;
           Aȝens þe feend þou make me   *against*
                stronge,
           And ȝyf me þy wyssynge;   *give   counsel*
           And þaȝ ich habbe y-do þe   *though I have*
                wrange,   *wrong*
84   Þou graunte me amendynge!

Shoreham has given us one of the rare examples in English of the figurative eulogy, a popular Latin genre.[11] He
emphasizes Mary at the focal point of human history
through preparation, act, and consequence. Events and
persons of the Old Testament prefigure the Incarnation
and Mary's virgin-maternity; at the center of history she
bears the Son of God; up to the poet's own time she
re-enacts her role in salvation by leading sinners to
heaven. History thus reflects the Incarnation in the past,
present, and future; all three times fuse into a present
reality by the reality of the Incarnation itself. The first
two parts of the poem—the introduction and the enumeration of Marian epithets with a *thou* anaphora—
converge in the final part, the petition proper. The introduction (stanzas one and two) presents the given situation: the speaker is a wretched sinner asking the Lady
Mary to overlook his dish of evil deeds and accept instead
the food of his prayers. A sinner in the presence of one
so noble cannot always express himself adequately. The
contrast between the speaker and the addressee might
also explain the aptness of the choice of genre: this song
is an enumeration of the accomplishments of a *lady* in
every sense of nobility. The distance between the two is
indeed great; what can a poor sinner say to praise such
a lady? St. Anselm found himself inadequate: "But what
shall I say? My tongue fails me because my intellect is
deficient" (III, 19). Or, as Ambrose Autpert, the speaker
might ask:

But what shall I, poor in ingenuity, say? whatever I shall speak of you is less praise than your worth deserves. If I call you a heaven, you are higher. If I say mother of the nations, you surpass it. If I call you the image of God, you are worthy. . . . How therefore shall I speak worthily of you, how shall I address you when a carnal tongue is inadequate to relate your virtues? In the meantime let the carnal tongue be silent in those praises which the soul always reveals ardently within ("De Festo Assumptionis," *PL*, XXXIX, 2131).

As St. Bonaventure realizes, Mary's excellencies are so great that even Scripture itself is deficient. Words alone cannot commend her adequately, so the Holy Spirit through the mouths of prophets praises her in figures— not by one, for that will not suffice, but by many.[12] Here indeed a solution suggests itself for our speaker's dilemma: since his own words cannot suffice, he can turn to those figures with which the Holy Spirit Himself has praised Mary's unutterable perfection. In our poem, then, the accumulation of figures underscores this perfection, just as the persistent anaphora heightens it verbally.

As the speaker explicitly states (line 4), his poem is a song, and Shoreham casts it in the form of address plus petition. Stanzas three and thirteen, the first and last stanzas of the enumeration proper, use this form to accentuate the fact that the epithets speak of Mary's role in salvation and thus form a basis for the petition. Taken as a whole, however, the poem divides into twelve stanzas of address and two of petition. The preponderance of address fits the psychological state of the wretched sinner addressing one so exalted; only after praising does he feel justified in petitioning. This tone involves a recognition of the states of both speaker and addressee; the speaker is keenly aware of the expanse which separates him from the Virgin. It thus indicates an appropriate spiritual attitude and justifies the petition. And finally, the tone suggests that the difficulty lies in finding words with which to praise Mary; once this difficulty is overcome, the speaker can make his request with absolute confidence that Mary will grant it. What he needs to concentrate on, then, is not the petition, but the address. As a song of praise, the poem repeats the two principal motifs announced in the opening line: Mary's mildness and nobility. Her mildness is implied in the figure of Judith (especially lines 41–42), Esther (especially lines 47–48), and the virgin in lines 65–66. It is more explicit in that of Emmaus (lines 57–58), and reappears explicitly in the petition proper (line 78). Mary's nobility is a more complex motif. It appears in the general sense of the word *leuedy* (lines 17, 71, 77, 79), in Mary's belonging to the royal house of David (line 24), in her being queen of Assuerus (line 44), possibly in her being the "ryche castel" (line 57), and in the woman in the Apocalypse (lines 67–72). But Mary's nobility includes more than these references indicate on the surface. The first recurrence of the nobility motif (lines 7–8) refers to her kingdom, and our poet has surely blundered in not making the lines read "Þou art quene of paradys, / Of erþe, *of hell,* of al þat hys," in keeping with Mary's title of Empress of Hell, and in keeping with the reference to Mary's power over the fiend throughout the poem. In lines 9–10 Mary's nobility is expanded by implicitly setting up the traditional reason for Mary's queenship: her bearing the King of Kings. This is done, as we have said, implicitly by the words *quene* and *kynge*. Mary's nobility, then, includes her role as Mother of Christ. The concept expands still further (line 10) to include Mary's sinlessness. Finally, the third occurrence of the anaphora suggests a relation to the other two clauses, and the concept of nobility includes her power over Satan. When our poet calls Mary "fre" (line 1), he refers to three aspects of her nobility: she is Mother of the Redeemer, an ab-

solutely sinless virgin, and victor over Satan. Since Mary
is Mother of the Redeemer, she has placated God's wrath
towards man; the poet thus uses the symbols of the dove
and the virgin in whose lap the unicorn lies. Her absolute
sinlessness often appears in the Middle Ages under the
image of spiritual beauty; moreover, since the exegetical
tradition of the Song of Songs equated physical with
spiritual beauty, Mary's beauty is often spoken of in
this double sense. Thus she appears in the poem as
Judith, Esther, and Rachel. Finally, Mary is instrumental
in defeating Satan, and the poet sees her role prefigured
in the stories of David, Judith, and Esther, and mirrored
in the figure of the woman in the Apocalypse.

Shoreham carefully ties together his introduction,
enumeration, and petition. In stanza two he prepares
for the enumeration by the allusion to Eve. Mary's bearing her Son without sin and pain (lines 9–10) separates
her not only from the rest of mankind—from the sinful
speaker, certainly—but especially from Eve, referred to
in lines 11–12. The contrast between Eve and the New
Eve recurs throughout the Middle Ages; Amedeus points
out the aspects relevant here: "Eve bore corrupt, Mary
brought forth incorrupt; Eve in sorrow, Mary in health"
("De Maria Virginea Matri," IV, *PL*, CLXXXVIII, 1323).
The implication here becomes explicit in Richard of St.
Victor:

> Sensual desire is the cause of sorrow, and sorrow the
> effect of sensual desire. . . . She who conceived in
> virginity conceived without sensual desire, and con-
> sequently is understood to have given birth without
> sorrow (*De Emmanuele*, I, 10, *PL*, CXCVI, 617–618).

Thus, Shoreham's use of Old Testament typology here
prepares for the figures which follow. Similarly, the last
stanza of the enumeration (lines 73–78) prepares for the
petition proper (lines 79–84) by concluding with a petition. Moreover, the petition proper echoes certain words

and ideas of the introduction. "Senfolle" (lines 78 and 80) recalls the reference (lines 5–6) to the speaker's evil deeds but frequent prayers (as does line 83). Further, "leuedy" (lines 77, 79) relates to "fre" (line 1) and to Mary's queenship (lines 7–8). Finally, by including two verbal echoes of the introduction ("mylde," lines 78 and 1; "songe," lines 79 and 4), the conclusion reminds us that the poem is a song of address and petition. The parallelism running throughout the poem effectively supports the song's thematic variation, and intensifies the speaker's emotion. This intensity in turn must have deepened the medieval audience's realization of Mary's qualities and position, and invited them to share the speaker's feelings. If the way this song develops has not proved contrapuntal enough for modern tastes, it has nonetheless an excellent and highly pleasing homophony.

Another ready-made form which the medieval poet could borrow from religious devotion was that of the meditation. The modern reader is likely to be more sympathetic toward this than toward the address-plus-petition formula, for the meditation marches smartly along from beginning to end—even if commanded by some predetermined numerical control like the seven heavenly joys of Mary or the seven sheddings of Christ's blood. The meditation usually breaks into two parts: first, a deliberation upon a scene, usually from the Gospel, and often presented in great detail; * second, such deliberation excites pious affections, which lead either to some appropriate resolution or to a petition for a special grace. The form itself is pliant enough to allow a variety in handling.

* Although a Gospel scene is the usual subject of the meditation in the religious lyrics, any subject may be chosen. "Merci abid an loke al day" (XIV, No. 61), for example, briefly meditates upon the quality of mercy and concludes with a petition. An interesting variation on the form of the meditation is one in which both the scene and the petition are part of Christ's appeal to man, e.g., "Man and wyman, loket to me" (XIV, No. 4).

Here, for example, is one section from the Hours of the
Cross (XIV, No. 30):

	Iesus, þat wald efter mid-night	*willed*
	Þi suete face, þat was sa bright,	
	With Iuus spitting file;	*to be defiled*
4	And suffer siþen, for vr sin,	
	Boffetes on þi soft chin,	
	In þat ilk quile;	*same time*
	Þat ilk tim þou fra ded ras,	*from death arose*
8	Lauerd godd, als þi will was,	
	Mildli and still;	
	Ken us, lauerd, for þi nam,	*Make us know*
	Forsak bat sin and scam	*both shame*
12	And vr werckes ill;	
	Of vr sinnes son to rise,	
	And wis us euer wit þe wise,	*guide*
	And leue vr gamens grill,	*harsh games*
16	Þat with þin apostels hei,	
	Mai þow all se in galilei,	*Galilee*
	If it be þi will.	

This particular version of the Hours of the Cross consists
of eight such meditations, each corresponding to a different event of the Passion, and each connected temporally with the canonical hours of the Divine Office.
Although our poet has handled the individual meditations with a fair degree of skill, he does not build satisfactorily to an emotional climax. The meditation at none
is the most intense, but the poet all but isolates it from
the preceding meditations. Although the effect of the
individual parts is often good, the chronological sequence
does not correlate with any emotional sequence. On the
other hand, "Ihesu, that alle this worlde hast wroghte"
(XV, No. 92), a meditation on the seven sheddings of
Christ's blood, does correlate the two much more suc-

cessfully. The poet divides his meditation into two parts: first, the seven sheddings, then seven appropriate petitions related to their respective scenes. The sense of accumulation which the second section creates intensifies the fervor of the petitions. This poet has clearly made the form of the meditation comply with what he has to say.

Devotion to the five joys of Mary, which bears a structural relationship to the meditation, is reflected throughout the course of the English lyric.[13] The form which this devotion ultimately took is illustrated in English by the twelfth-century *Ancrene Riwle;* here the meditation upon each joy is divided into two parts, in which, to quote Dom André, "le mystère joyeux est énoncé" and "une pétition appropriée fait suite" (p. 335). In the next century Stephen of Salley divided his meditations into three parts: the actual meditation, the enumeration of the joy, and a petition (p. 339). The poets who treat this same subject fashion their materials with varying dexterity. Sometimes they merely enumerate the joys and omit the petition ("The ferste joye, as I you telle," Greene, No. 231). Sometimes they follow each joy with a petition ("Seinte marie, leuedi brist," XIII, No. 18). Sometimes they enumerate all the joys, then conclude with the petition ("Ase y me rod þis ender day," XIV, No. 11). And one poet not only uses the twofold structure, but adds one introductory and three concluding stanzas of petition ("Heyl be þou, marie, milde quene of heuene," XIV, No. 26). Finally, the oldest poem on the joys, the Latin "Gaude virgo, mater Christi," merely enumerates the joys with a *Gaude* anaphora; the English translator, however, felt the tradition of the twofold meditative structure, for he turns *Gaude* into a petition, "Glade us" (XIII, No. 22). But by the fifteenth century the tradition weakened, and numerous poems were written without a petition.

Using the joys as a devotional exercise, "Haile be þu, mari, maiden bright" (XIV, No. 31) illustrates how the meditative form can be made to comply with the poet's thought. It centers in the meditation; the first two stanzas introduce the exercise, and the last four serve as conclusion. The sorrowful speaker intends this meditation as an act of devotion—a prayer within a prayer with a proven efficacy. The meditation over, he beseeches Mary for immediate aid, asking her to intercede with her divine Son. Convinced of her might, he reminds himself, as proof of her power, that when he names her sweet name, he makes the devils flee (lines 51–55). In this passage his confidence increases, so that by line 56 he finds consolation for his sorrow from his meditation upon the joys. His mood, then, shifts from sorrow to joy (line 57), and the central section of the poem provides the transition. The remaining lines repeat motifs from the opening stanzas; the repetition gains in significance because the tone has shifted to joy. Aside from this important change in tone, the poem makes use of another cohesive device; the introductory stanzas herald a vassal-lady motif, which sweeps through the conclusion. The speaker resolves to sin no more and commends his entire being to Mary (lines 8–10); this pledge of the vassal effects Mary's protection. By his meditation upon the joys, the sinner performs a kind of feudal homage preparatory to his actual request for protection in the final stanzas. He introduces each petition within the meditation with *leuedi,* which gains a particular relevance within the context. As one of Mary's retinue (line 50) the speaker now asks for her protection against the severe onslaughts of the devil (lines 51–52). The next two lines continue the notion of warfare and the lady's protection. *Spere* in line 59 Brown glosses as "hope" (XIV, p. 348); this connects the line with line 53, and is a familiar Marian epithet. In the context, however, the poet surely puns on the word also as *spear*, i.e., "defense," and thus relates it to *were* in line 60.[14] The concluding stanza, then, completes the dramatizing of the vassal-lady relationship.

We have seen how our poet assimilates the meditation upon the joys into other controlling forms; we shall now look more closely at his technique within the meditation proper. He varies his presentation of the joys: he visualizes the Annunciation scene in great detail; he considers the Nativity figuratively; he summarizes and comments on the Epiphany; he summarily juxtaposes the Resurrection and the Crucifixion; and finally, he alludes to certain events associated with the Assumption. The first joy manages its biblical materials wisely; it begins suddenly with "Þar" (line 11), and we are immediately at the scene of the Annunciation. In lines 11–12 our attention focuses on Mary, but only as a secondary actor in the scene, introduced in a subordinate adverbial clause.* The main clause begins with line 13, and our attention shifts to the angel come from heaven. Gabriel is the main actor in this stanza, but his greeting shifts our attention back to Mary. In stanza four the roles reverse: Gabriel is still present, but we do not hear his message. Instead, we see Mary's reaction ("Stil þu stod," line 16) and hear her unhesitating ("ne stint þu noght," line 16) confession of her great humility: "Al his wil it sal be wroght / in his ancele" (lines 18–19). The scene concludes as quickly as it began. These two stanzas recount the event vividly and briefly; all we have is the beginning and the end of the scene. Gabriel's greeting is the poet's own invention and not scriptural, yet it suggests Gabriel's entire message. The poet follows tradition in his image describing the Nativity and in his interpretation of the gifts of the Magi. He does more than merely enumerate these two joys, however; the image

* Line 11, however, may be interpreted as an independent clause.

in the first comments upon some theological implications of the Incarnation, and in the second the speaker contemplates the significance of the scene. In other words, the meditation does not decrease in intensity from the detail of the opening scene. The poet joins the Crucifixion with his mention of the Resurrection in order to accentuate Mary's joy. The Assumption stanza alludes in line 42 to popular tradition: "Þe iuus [Jews] þe soght and fand þe noght"; the line is paralleled, e.g., in the Coptic version of the Assumption and in a Nestorian legend.[15] The petitions with which the speaker concludes each meditation vary in their applicability to their respective joys. The first and fifth apply very well; the other three, however, dangle loosely from their meditations. All five of them do reflect the initial mood of the speaker, and they anticipate the petitions of the concluding stanzas. Moreover, the entire poem is cast into a general address-petition structure, with stanzas one to nine forming the address, and ten to thirteen the petition. This over-all structure fits the vassal-lady relationship in its structure of commendation and request for protection. The various elements of this poem, then, combine into a well-knit whole and demonstrate that the poet has bent his pre-existing religious forms to the inclination of his thought.

Another example of the organic handling of the meditative structure combines it with the literary form of the *débat;* in "Stond wel, moder, vnder rode" (XIII, No. 49B), the "contestants" are Christ and Mary. Jesus continually reminds His Mother of the spiritual import of His death, while Mary is the Mother who sees her only Son die the ignominious death of the cross (lines 29–30). This *débat* structure is one of the devices the poet employs to emphasize the tender Mother-Son relationship. The poem begins with an almost paradoxical injunction of Christ's:

> "Stond wel, moder, vnder rode;
> bihold þi child wyth glade
>   mode,
> blyþe, moder, mittu ben."   *may you be*

To which Mary replies:

> 4   "Svne, quu may bliþe stonden?
> hi se þin feet, hi se þin honden,
>   nayled to þe harde tre."

Having set up this conflict between Jesus and Mary, the poet uses it to excellent advantage in the following lines:

> "Moder, reu vpon þi bern!   *child*
> þu wasse awey þo blodi teren,   *wash*
> 15   it don me werse þan mi ded."   *death*

The ambiguity of line 13 gives the stanza a strong undercurrent of irony: Christ's request arises from the very fact that Mary does have pity upon her Child, and the wording of this request serves to increase the pathos of the scene. Also to underscore the pathos and invite the reader's compassion, our poet repeats certain key words and ideas with strong emotional appeal, especially *Mother* and *Son,* which begin the respective speeches.*
The strict stanzaic division into two halves of the debate, although contributing to the emotional value, also helps to curb the emotion. So strict a division might seem at first to overformalize the poem; we might wish for some irregularity in stanzaic division to increase the intensity. But the balance which the poet's division gives keeps the poem from many of the excesses often associated with the Franciscan school.

The poem falls into two distinct sections: the dialogue proper (stanzas one to nine) and the petition

---

* Others are *þole,* appearing four times, *pain* thrice, *pained* once; *sorrow* twice, *sorry* once; *rue* twice, *rueful* once; *care* and *woe* each once; *tears* twice, *weeping* once; *death* six times, *die* five times.

(stanzas ten and eleven). The transition between sections is rather abrupt, but we can defend the petition on a number of grounds. First, the petition opposes Mary's joy at the Resurrection with her sorrow at the Crucifixion. Second, the petition has been prepared for by lines 46–48, in which Mary intercedes for her spiritual children. And the speaker makes his petition in words appropriate to the Crucifixion: "Moder, for þat hithe [precious] blode / þat he sadde [shed] vpon þe rode" (lines 64–65). And third, the thought division of our poem corresponds to that of a meditation: the first section visualizes the scene in detail, and a petition follows, based upon the preceding visualization. Within the given formal restrictions, our poet builds a strong characterization of Mary, a portrayal important in the development of the theme and in uniting the last two stanzas with the rest of the poem. Until stanza twelve Mary's role as Mother of Christ has included only a recognition of the sufferings of her Son; now she realizes that her role involves much more. She must become reconciled to His divine mission and recognize that she is Mother of the Redeemer. Thus she is able to request:

> "Sune, help alle at nede,
> alle þo þat to me greden—   *cry*
> 48   m[ay]den, wyf, and fol wyman."

At this point Christ may now depart for limbo, where He will redeem Adam (lines 49–51). The identification of Mother and Son is complete in the next lines: "Sune, y wyle wi' the funden [go], / y [deye ywis] of þine wnden" (lines 52–53). Christ has reminded Mary that her role as Mother must enable Him to undergo the descent into Hell—a rebirth, so that now for the first time Mary must undergo the birth pangs which she had forfeited earlier (lines 37–39). Part of these birth pangs is a renunciation of her role as Mother of the man Christ and recognition of her role as bearer of the Redeemer. Mary realizes this, unites herself with her Son by willing to go *with* Him, not die *before* Him, as in line 36. Only in this way can she become Mother of mankind. This transformation, then, anticipates the speaker's request in the second part that Mary be our shield against our foe (line 60). Only through Mary's recognition of her proper maternal role can the speaker beseech her for delivery from Hell. And by emphasizing Mary's role as Mother of mankind, the poet utilizes his meditative structure organically to heighten his audience's consciousness of Mary's place in salvation.

To be successful, the meditative structure should ideally offer some kind of interpretation of the biblical event which it considers. The speaker should somehow become involved in the poem, either directly, or indirectly through the freshness of the interpretation. Emphases differ from poem to poem; some stress the scene, others emphasize the speaker's reactions. Some poems, however, concentrate only on the speaker's emotional involvement in the scene; they do not present any petition, and therefore do not share the general meditative structure. Such poems may have been influenced by the meditation, or they may not; we cannot, of course, be certain. One example of this type of poem we have already seen, "Þe minde of þi passiun" (XIII, No. 56); another example presents more of the scene as well as the speaker's emotion (XIII, No. 1). In fact, the scene and the speaker's reactions are so closely interwoven that the speaker seems actually to be a spectator at the scene.[16]

> Nou goth sonne vnder wod—
> me reweth, marie, þi faire Rode.   *complexion*
> Nou goþ sonne vnder tre—
> 4   me reweþ, marie, þi sone and
>   þe.

The poem consists of two succeeding scenes, which the poet has intensified by limiting them spatially and temporally in themselves, and by contrasting them spatially and temporally. The first scene (lines 1–2) is viewed close up: the sun sinks behind a part of the cross—possibly an arm, as Kane suggests (p. 140)—while Mary keeps her lonely vigil. The poet's use of grammatical coordination suggests a relationship in thought between the sun's setting and his own regret for Mary's complexion: the red of the sunset is reflected in Mary's face, and for this marring of the Virgin's beauty the poet grieves. I agree with Brown that this line depends upon the clause from Songs i.5, "quia decoloravit me sol" (p. 166), and I see no suggestion, as does John Cutler, that Mary has been sunburnt from her long vigil "beside the dying Christ, heedless of the sun's rays which have burned her face." [17] The discoloration comes rather from the red of the sunset; here the poet has parted from his source. Nor do I agree with Kane that line 2 is "half impertinent, secular . . . scarcely pious; it is the poet's perennial regret for beauty destroyed" (p. 140). The line is in perfect keeping with the emotional emphasis of what becomes the Franciscan school. I find line 2 close to, but more specific and profound than, these lines from the "Stabat Mater Dolorosa":

> Quis est homo qui non fleret
> Matrem Christi si videret
> In tanto supplicio?
> Quis non posset contristari
> Christi Matrem contemplari
> Dolentem cum Filio?

Further emotional appeal lies in the setting of the sun, which relates to the traditional comparison of grief to night, as well as to the suggestion of "a long day of immeasurable unhappiness." [18] In the final two lines our poet presents a second scene, which contrasts spatially and temporally with the first. The opening word *nou* indicates a lapse of time—the sun has almost set—and this intensifies the emotion. In this second scene the poet has expanded his picture: we see at a distance the entire cross with Jesus transfixed, Mary beside it, and the sun disappearing behind it. This expansion of the scene intensifies the Mother-Son relationship.

In addition to the actual sunset, the image refers to Christ; it is a commonplace symbol of divinity. In fact, two copyists read the image only as *Son:* a garbled version in Harley 1121 reads: "Now goth godes son vnder wode," and Sloane 2275 reads: "Now gose þi son undur wode . . . Now gose þi son undur tre." [19] Furthermore, the chief source of the poem, Songs i.5 with its attendant verse i.4, was interpreted by Philippe of Harvengt and John Halgrinus as meaning that Mary was overcome by sorrow at seeing her Son on the cross and shared her Son's ignominy.[20] Philippe discusses Mary's sufferings, and in addition to pointing out the human relationship, tells us that part of the Mother's suffering arose from her knowledge that it is the Son of God Himself Whom the scoffers are crucifying (col. 225). Later on, Philippe puns on *sol* (Mary is speaking): "Ille inquam Sol qui respectu vultus sui cuncta reficit et decorat, sua quadam absentia me ad modicum decolorat" (col. 231). John Halgrinus also puns on *sol:*

> *Nigra sum,* despecata, offuscata, obscurata, decolorata, *quia decoloravit me sol* moriens; decolorem me fecit sol obscuratus et offuscatus: de qua solis offuscatione et obscuratione dicit Isais, loquens de Christi passione: 'Non est species neque decor. . . .' In passione enim in Christo non apparuit species vel decor majestatis, sed quasi leprosus, ob similitudinem carnis peccati reputatus est [Is. liii.2, 4];

and again: "Nam ideo *fusca sum,* quia *decoloravit me sol,* cui in passione sua 'non fuit species neque decor. . . .' " These interpretations are very similar to those of the passage from Ruth mentioned in the Digby MS (XIII, p. 165). They also clarify the structural importance of the sun image in our poem: it is Mary's Son Who is dying, and just as the red of the actual sunset is reflected in Mary's face, marring her beauty, so also is the death of her Son reflected in Mary's face. In this way the poet underscores Mary's participation in Christ's suffering. The sun image makes us aware also that God Himself is dying and that the relationship between Mary and Jesus is not merely Mother-Son. Finally, our poet has happily substituted redness for the darkness in Canticles, for since red is the color of love, the symbol of the sunset combines both the grief and love which Mary felt for her dying Son. The poet has thus taken a simple, surface emotion aroused by the Crucifixion scene and has made it profound, by use of symbol, by the sensuous details of the setting, by a contrast in space and time between lines 3–4 and 1–2, and by the sound value of its linear structure.

"Nou goth sonne vnder wod" represents beautifully the kind of Middle English lyric that many modern critics prefer—lyrics which concentrate on the speaker's emotional involvement in the subject, and which follow some kind of logical progression. Lyrics which are not so characterized—including many of those we have considered in this chapter—modern critics tend to find formless and unappealing. On the other hand, they are as prone to find just as distasteful those lyrics which do adhere strictly to a clear-cut form such as the meditation. Apparently there is nothing so bad as a medieval lyric which is formless, unless it's a medieval lyric which is formalized. We cannot exonerate a medieval poet's mechanical handling of his form, but certainly we must be conscious of how much or how little form he is actually using before we decide it is mechanical. A ready-made religious form such as the meditation is comparatively easy to evaluate, but the address-plus-petition form is not so easy. While the presentation of the scene in the meditation requires some kind of logical progression, the address-plus-petition formula is based on emotion rather than logic. In a given poem this formula may indeed be mechanical, or it may mimetically reproduce a particular psychological condition. The formlessness, if you will, is part of the psychological state which the poet imitates. An age which is accustomed to the stream-of-consciousness technique should not be particularly disturbed by the so-called lack of unity created by the wandering thoughts of a medieval sinner as he recalls one Marian image after another. May not a poet choose this method to portray the deficiency a sinner feels when he addresses one so exalted as the Blessed Virgin Mary, the Mother of God Himself? But the stream-of-conscious-ness technique differs from the medieval poet's char-acter analysis in one immediately important aspect: the psychological analysis which the medieval poet presents does not tend to be as intimate, as unique as the modern author's. The medieval poet is restricted in the depth of his analysis both by his audience's expectations and by the nature of the *song* which he is composing. Our investigation of the religious forms seems to lead us to the conclusion that many of the lyrics are comparatively formless. Yet such formlessness may be the very means the poet has chosen to convey his speaker's emotions. Not all the religious lyrics are as formless as many in this chapter; obviously, the lyrics utilize structures other than religious. Sometimes, as "Nou goth sonne" and "In a valey of þis restles mynde" demonstrate, the structure may be partially determined by the imagery. The nature and the importance of the imagery which the medieval poets used is the concern of the following chapter.

1. "The Music of Poetry," *Partisan Review,* IX (1942), 463–464.

2. Brown and Robbins, *Index,* p. 272, list 17 MSS in which the former appears. The latter appears in 50 versions, 19 of which exist independently of the *Speculum Christiani.*

3. *Mysticism* (New York, 1955), p. 76.

4. *"Orationes sive meditationes* quae subscriptae sunt, quoniam ad excitandam legentis mentem ad dei amorem vel timorem, seu ad suimet discussionem editae sunt, non sunt legendae in tumultu, sed in quiete, nec cursim et velociter, sed paulatim cum intenta et morosa meditatione. Nec debet intendere lector ut quamlibet earum totam perlegat, sed quantum sentit sibi deo adiuvante valere ad accendendum affectum orandi, vel quantum illum delectat. Nec necesse habet aliquam semper a principio incipere, sed ubi magis illi placuerit," *Opera Omnia,* ed. Francis S. Schmitt (Edinburgh, 1946), III, 3.

5. Printed in *Political, Religious, and Love Songs,* ed. Frederick J. Furnivall, EETS, XV (London, 1903), pp. 180–188.

6. Underhill, pp. 227–228.

7. See also Walter Hilton, *The Goad of Love,* ed. Clare Kirchberger (London, 1952), pp. 48–54. This treatise stresses the devotion to the Passion which is typical of mystic writings.

8. Pp. 150–151. The quotations which follow are from Suso, *Leben,* xxii, quoted by Underhill, p. 406; Tauler, Sermon for the 4th Sunday in Lent, *ibid.,* p. 396.

9. Printed in *The Poems of William Dunbar,* ed. W. Mackay Mackenzie (Edinburgh, 1932), pp. 160–161.

10. Printed by H. C. Schulz, "Middle English Texts from the 'Bement' Manuscript," *HLQ,* III (1939–40), 460–465.

11. The term is Erich Auerbach's; see his discussion of the genre in "Dante's Prayer to the Virgin (Paradiso, XXXIII) and Earlier Eulogies," *Romance Philology,* III (1949–50), 1–26. Although Shoreham generally uses well-known figures, some may still need explanation.

Lines 5–6: The unclean vessel and the prepared food are allusions to a miracle of the Virgin entitled by H. L. D. Ward "Dainties in a Foul Dish." He summarizes the miracle thus: "How a licentious clerk was visited on his sick-bed by the Virgin, who offered him three pears on a foul dish, as an emblem of his frequent prayers accompanied by evil deeds": *Catalogue of Romances in the Department of MSS in the British Museum* (London, 1893), II, 651.

Line 19: The burning bush (Ex. iii.2) is one of the favorite symbols of poet and preacher alike. Chaucer's Prioress addresses the Virgin in the prologue to her tale as "O bussh unbrent, brennynge in Moyses sighte" (line 468), and Chaucer himself explains the figure in his *ABC,* lines 89–94. The image has a further implication; the *Speculum of Gy de Warewycke* interprets the fire as concupiscence, and the fact that the bush did not burn indicates that "Hete of flesh ne mihte hire wemme": ed. Georgiana Morril, EETS ES, LXXV (London, 1898), p. 18.

Line 20: Sarah, like most women in the Old Testament, was considered a type of Mary. Brown glosses *rytte* as *legitimate*, as opposed to Hagar, Sarah's bondswoman (XIV, p. 256). Isaac was early seen as a type of Christ, so the identification of Sarah with Mary was natural. The uniqueness of both conceptions is mentioned by a fourteenth-century poet who addresses Mary: "Rejoice, O singular Sarah, / By the sacred word you shall be made fecund" (*AH*, XV, No. 120).

Line 24: Mary's belonging to the house of David is frequently mentioned in the figurative eulogies, often in connection with her royalty. As Richard of St. Lawrence explains, "She was of a tribe both priestly and royal: because she brought forth Christ, who is both king and priest." (Modern scholars attribute to him the *De Laudibus Beatae Virginis Mariae*, found in St. Albert the Great, *Opera Omnia*, ed. Augustus and Aemilius Borgnet [Paris, 1890–99], XXXVI. The passage quoted occurs in VI.xiii.3, p. 354A.) Reference to her ancestry also connotes Mary's role as Mother of the Redeemer, for it was well known that the Messiah would be of the house of David (see, e.g., Matt. xxii.42).

Lines 27–30: Aaron's rod is one of the most widely used figures in the eulogies and sermons alike. The figure is taken from Num. xvii.8. Shoreham follows the accepted interpretation and compares the miraculous nature of the rod's blooming with Mary's giving birth to Christ and remaining a virgin. Numerous poets and preachers pun on *virga* and *virgo*, as Auerbach notes (p. 12).

Line 31: The Blessed Virgin is here called the temple of Solomon; variants of this image are the house, throne, and bed of Solomon. Reasons for the aptness of this symbol are offered by a number of authors. To Richard of St. Lawrence, e.g., Mary is a temple because through her we direct prayers to Christ; further, the habitation of God is the temple, and Mary was the habitation of Christ (*De Laudibus*, X.xxii.1, p. 523A–B). Often this image was discussed in great detail, various parts of the temple corresponding to Mary's virtues.

Line 32: The fleece in the story of Gideon is another of the most popular figures of the virgin birth. The figure is taken from Judges vi.36–38. The fleece, dew, and dry area are, respectively, the Virgin, the grace of the Holy Spirit by which she conceived, and her intact virginity.

Lines 37–43: Judith is another popular Old Testament type of Mary, although the story is seldom referred to in the figurative eulogy with the detail our author gives it. *Fayre wyf* (line 37) is based on references to Judith's beauty (e.g., viii.7, x.4, 14). Line 42 M. Konrath would translate as "That to the well come" in

Poems of William of Shoreham, EETS ES, LXXXVI (London, 1902), p. 236. He argues that *by-nome* in line 40 is second person singular, preterite indicative, and historically has a long *o*. Since *come* (line 42) rimes with it, it must be the preterite plural, and *wylle* cannot be the verb. He finds justification for translating *wylle* as *well* on the basis of Judith vii.6. However, the vowel of the past participle (*u*) had very likely been extended into the preterite of *binimen*, and *by-nome* would therefore rime with *come*, the infinitive. Furthermore, the reference to the well in Judith does not seem to fit this context. The line may therefore be translated, "That to thee will come."

Lines 43–48: Esther was considered a fitting type of Mary chiefly for three reasons, all of which our poet incorporates into his stanza: her beauty ("þat swete þynge," line 43), the love of Assuerus (i.e., Christ, lines 44–46), and her saving her people (i.e., mankind, lines 47–48).

Lines 49–52: The prophecy of Ezechiel (xliv. 2–3) is one of the oldest and most widespread Marian texts in the Western church. The closed gate means that Mary's virginity remained intact before, during, and after her giving birth to Christ.

Lines 53–54: The beauty of Rachel (Gen. xxix.17) was the usual basis for her being a type of Mary.

Lines 55–56: Another very popular figure is the mountain of Daniel ii.34. The stone cut from the mountain without hands is Christ, Who was born of the Virgin Mary without the arms of embraces.

Lines 57–60: Emmaus is an unusual figure; I have found no other occurrence of it. The author's use of it, moreover, is curious. The reference is to Luke xxiv.13. Shoreham's *castel* is the usual rendering of Latin *castellum*, "village"; *castel* in this sense may be found in Old English, although in Middle English, as the NED notes, it was often understood in the more familiar sense of a fortified residence. *Ryche* in line 57 is used in the sense of "noble," "exalted," as it could mean in Old English with reference to persons. Here it is extended to a place: the *castel* is *ryche* because of the presence of Christ. In line 58 what our poet had in mind was probably the invitation of the two disciples to Jesus to stay with them, apparently for refreshment (xxiv.29–30). Possibly this passage led the poet to assume that Emmaus was a resting place for travelers. The epithet may refer to the town as it existed in the Middle Ages. After the Crusades, four places claimed to be the Emmaus of the Gospel; see Giuseppe Ricciotti, *The Life of Christ* (Milwaukee, 1947), p. 656 n. There is possibly also a connection with another frequent image, also from Luke (x.38): "And He [Jesus] entered into a certain castle [i.e., village]," viz., Bethany, the home of Mary and Martha. The castle, according to glosses on this passage, is the Blessed Virgin Mary. Lines 59–60 are connected with the Emmaus figure by the passage quoted above, where Jesus stopped and broke bread with His disciples. The reference in line 60 is to the very famous prophecy of Is. vii.14.

Line 62: This is probably to be explained in terms of the difference between the Old and New Dispensations; the God of the Old Testament was a God of justice and fear, while the God of the New is One of love. It has reference also to the Son's offering satisfaction to the Father for the sin of Adam by His humbling Himself in His incarnation and passion.

Lines 63–66: Here reference is made to the legendary unicorn, which in the *physiologi* symbolized Christ. A good parallel is found in Philippe de Thaun's bestiary, ed. Emmanuel Walbert (Lund, 1900), pp. 15–17. Another very close parallel (in English) is lines 25–32 of the *Meditations on the Life and Passion of Christ*, ed. Charlotte D'Evelyn, EETS, CLVIII (London, 1920).

Lines 67–72: The woman in Rev. xii.1 was commonly interpreted as Mary, but the details seem to have had no standard interpretation.

12. "De Nativitate Beatae Virginis Mariae," II, *Opera Omnia* (Quaracchi, 1901), IX, 708A–B. For the topos of inexpressibility, see Ernst R. Curtius, *European Literature and the Latin Middle Ages*, trans. Willard R. Trask (New York, 1953), pp. 159–162.

13. For the history of this devotion, see André Wilmart, *Auteurs spirituels et textes dévots du moyen-âge latin* (Paris, 1932), pp. 331–336.

14. The image of the shield occurs more frequently than that of the spear; for the latter, however, cf. lines 20815–18 of the same MS of the *Cursor Mundi* from which this poem is taken.

15. In the Coptic version the Apostles carry Mary's body to the tomb for burial; the Jews are heard singing and have come to burn the body. They are repulsed by a wall of fire which encompasses the Apostles, and the Jews are blinded. The Apostles then lay the body in the tomb and, following Jesus' command, keep vigil for three and a half days. The Jews, in terror, confess their sins and ask pardon. They are cured of their blindness, but when they search the tomb for the body of Mary, they cannot find it. Amazed, they confess themselves guilty. In the Nestorian version, the Jews make several attempts to attack the body of Mary, and on their last attempt they open the tomb and find it empty. Several are immediately converted, but the others remain unbelieving and fight among themselves for possession of Mary's clothing. See

Montague R. James, *The Apocryphal New Testament* (Oxford, 1926), p. 196; Martin Jugie, *La Mort et l'Assomption de la Sainte Vierge*, Studi e Testi, CXIV (Vatican City, 1944), p. 126.

16. The following explication first appeared in *MLN*, LXXIV (1959), 578–581, and is reprinted here with minor changes with the kind permission of the Johns Hopkins Press.

17. "Nou Goth Sonne Vnder Wod," *Explicator*, IV (1945), item 7.

18. Kane, p. 140. Cf. XIII, No. 47:

> þe brithe day went in-to nith
> þo ihesu crist þin herte lith
> 12   was iqueint with pine and wo.

19. Brown, *Register*, I, 310, 376.

20. *PL*, CCIII, 224–225; *PL*, CCVI, 84–86.

CHAPTER FOUR

ANALOGY AND IMAGERY

To a degree that many moderns cannot appreciate, the medieval world was theocentric. It was theocentric spatially and temporally—i.e., in the realm of nature and in the realm of history. Nature was a theophany; it was the visible garment of divinity; it was, as Emile Mâle points out,

> a book written by the hand of God in which every creature is a word charged with meaning. The ignorant see the forms—the mysterious letters—understanding nothing of their meaning, but the wise pass from the visible to the invisible, and in reading nature read the thoughts of God. True knowledge, then, consists not only in the study of things in themselves—the outward forms—but in penetrating to the inner meaning intended by God for our instruction, for in the words of Honorius of Autun, "every creature is a shadow of truth and life." [1]

This concept of the correspondence between the visible and the invisible, the corporeal and the spiritual, has a long history, but in the later Middle Ages it was vitalized by St. Francis of Assisi and especially by St. Bonaventure in his celebrated doctrine of analogy.[2] When we consider the significant role of the Franciscans in shaping English spirituality and especially in shaping the course of the English lyric, the wonder is that this doctrine of analogy and its role in the symbolic interpretation of the universe inspired so few of the English religious lyrics. But if God spoke to man through nature, he spoke also through history. For the Christian, all history unites at its focal point: the Incarnation and Redemption; as Mâle says, "All leads up to Christ as all begins anew in Him" (p. 176). To read the Old Testament is to accept the events which it narrates as historical facts; to read it from the focal point of history is to interpret these facts as prophecies. The concept of a *New* Testament which abrogated the Old meant that the Old in itself had application only for the Jews and not for the Christians; exegetes, therefore, following the example of St. Paul and indeed of Christ Himself, gave the Old Testament a Christian relevance.[3] Similarly, profane history was given a Christian reference and was interpreted as reflecting the Old Testament or the New. But the Incarnation was not only the fulfillment of the old dispensation; it began the new. It embodied a set of spiritual values which affect the daily life of the Christian throughout time. It embodied a spiritual reality which was given meaning in the interior life of every Christian. The Incarnation therefore has for the Christian a profundity which transcends its historical reality. As Jean Daniélou has remarked,

> The Christian faith has but one object: the mystery of Christ dead and risen. But this one only mystery subsists under different modes. It is prefigured in the Old Testament; it is realized historically in the life of Christ on earth; it is contained by way of mystery in the sacraments; it is lived mystically in souls; it is accomplished socially in the Church;

it is consummated eschatologically in the kingdom
of heaven. Thus the Christian has at his disposal,
for the expression of that single reality, several regis-
ters, a symbolism of several dimensions. All Christian culture consists in grasping the bonds of union
that exist between the Bible and liturgy, between
the Gospel and eschatology, between the mystical
life and the liturgy.[4]

Thus, in history as well as in nature, behind the surface,
lay the invisible reality which unified all human existence.

    This unity of existence, which so characterizes me-
dieval thought, echoes in the religious lyrics in several
ways. Given such a view of existence, we will not be
surprised to find that the medieval poets saw an analogy
between the Virgin Mary and the lady of troubadour
love song and chivalric romance. In the Middle Ages
the two influences—religious and secular—are always
coalescing, and the analogies between the secular and
the religious worked both ways. The Church always
seized upon ingrained and popular customs and transformed them for her own purposes; literature written
under her guidance shows the same phenomenon. St.
Francis himself was "God's troubadour" and transformed
courtly traditions for his special spiritual purpose. But
the catalogues of passages which commentators insist on
displaying to prove the influence of courtly love on the
Marian lyric are awfully dispiriting. They could better
devote themselves to explaining the extent to which a
certain passage deliberately imitates secular love song,
and to what purpose this borrowing serves in the poem
as a whole, especially to what degree it affects the tone.
Contrary to some opinions, the tone in the Marian lyric
rarely duplicates that in the secular; Patterson's "com-
pensatory" theory at least amuses. Picture the lonely
monks in their cells, unconsciously seeking to offset their

vows of celibacy by pouring forth their souls in lyric
cries to the Virgin Mary. Sir Philip Sidney might easily
have been thinking of such poems when he complained:
"But truly, many of such writings as come under the
banner of unresistible love, if I were a mistress would
never persuade me they were in love." [5] Modern commentators object to this very inconsistency between tone
and content when they stigmatize such poems as *insin-
cere*—a devastating judgment, for according to this school
of criticism, no matter how crude the poems, the poets
themselves were at least sincere. But the fifteenth-century
poets who sang of Mary often worked within a tradition
which marked them off from that represented by the
intensity of earlier prayers to Mary in prose, such as
those of St. Anselm. The Marian poets attempted to
adopt a tradition of refined emotion, of self-analysis
which the troubadours before them had transformed
into successful lyrics, but which they seemed unable to
transform. They employed the more superficial troubadour conventions, letting these emerge in the Marian
poetry as an idealized form; that is, when the court poets
wrote their lyrics in praise of Mary they automatically
let these conventions formulate of themselves the speaker's emotion. The religious poets borrowed the more
obvious aspects of the troubadour self-analysis; they
seemed to prefer a gracefulness, a gentleness, indeed a
gentility which a strong personal element would violate.
Their preference for these qualities is perhaps best explained as another manifestation of their sense of de-
corum. The stanza form, the aureate diction, the alliteration—all manifest this cumulated tradition of propriety
which the fifteenth-century poets valued. The lack of
subjectivity, the pallid emotion, the conventionalized
sentiments in praise of Mary thus merged with other aspects of the courtly tradition—a tradition which the
ordinary court poet would not think of abandoning and
could not transcend.

Some commentators have exaggerated the French influence on the English Marian lyric, but today we recognize how limited that influence actually is.[6] Patterson, for example, feels that in the English lyrics the tone is the same as in the troubadours'. On the contrary, the speakers in the English lyrics do realize Mary's role in man's redemption, and they beseech her to intercede with her Son on their behalf. The vassal-lord relationship is one aspect of secular custom which the Church uses as an ideal analogy for the relationship between the sinner and Mary. Examine the Marian lyrics and notice how often the speaker pledges his fidelity to Mary's service, offering her the flattery appropriate to an earthly lady, but *in exchange for* her protection against the devil or for being led into heaven.* This use of the vassal-lord relationship differs markedly from that in courtly love, where the lady acknowledges no obligation toward her vassal. Moreover, the authors of some of these Marian lyrics were not merely attempting to "sublimate earthly love" (Brook, p. 16). Some undoubtedly were. But others were steeped in the historical-psychological-symbolical Virgin as mother-spouse of Christ, as *Sophia,* as *anima,* as *Ecclesia.* They knew that the soul of man must be a Mary, a God-bearer; that man must, in fact, if he seeks perfection, repeat Mary's dual role—give birth to Christ within his heart and join himself with Christ in spiritual marriage. The poets knew too that as Mother, through whom her spiritual children are spiritually reborn, and as spouse of Christ, Mary also typifies the Church.[7] It is therefore possible at times to discern a separate ecclesiastical tradition in some Marian lyrics which happen to share the language of courtly love, for such lyrics reveal an awareness of Mary's ambivalence.

Perhaps the best example of such lyrics is "Cristes milde moder, seynte marie" ("On God Ureisun of Ure

* We have already noted this in "Haile be þu, mari, maiden bright" (XIV, No. 31).

Lefdi," XIII, No. 3). Here Mary as historical person blends with her peculiar office in the scheme of salvation: Mary not only bestows the graces by which man may come to terms with himself, confess his sins, and start anew, but also symbolizes the state itself. Fittingly, then, the poet addresses her as light and its various attributes. She is, in a real sense, *Sophia,* as the liturgy insists. By seeking union with her, man wishes to be guided by this ideal. But in that Mary is also mother, so that man may be reborn through her, she typifies the motherhood of God Himself. Gerald Vann has commented in this connection:

> We say "Mother of God, pray for us, sinners"; but it is essentially in order that through growing in love and understanding of the motherhood of Mary we may be led to know and love and adore, to accept and so be renewed by, the creative motherhood of God.[8]

St. Paul often speaks of being renewed in Christ; put off the old man, he tells the Ephesians, "And be renewed in the spirit of your mind: And put on the new man" (iv.22–24). Mary's role in our poem is exactly this renewal: "ʒif þu wult ðet ich iðeo, gode ʒeme nim to me / Vor wel ne wurð me neuer bute hit beo þuruh ðe" [if you wish me to prosper, take good heed to me/ For I will never become well unless it be through you] (lines 121–122). Mary's role as physician to the ailing sinner thus mirrors her role in rebirth: "of mine liue ʒif me lune" [grant me the gift of my life] (line 126), and earlier, "Vor o ðe is al ilong mi lif & eke min heale" [for in you is all along my life and also my health-salvation] (line 96). It is because the speaker realizes the role of Mary-Sophia that he brings himself into her bondage (lines 97–98); he must yield to her love, giving her "al mi suluen" (line 100), abandoning himself completely to the pursuit of the ideal for which she stands. But the image of the vassal-lady relationship (not the courtly lover-beloved, for Mary is much too generous for the beloved, lines 32 ff.) does not adequately express the relationship that must exist between Mary and the soul; the speaker therefore expresses it more forcibly: "Mi lif is þin, mi luue is þin, mine heorte blod is þin, / and ʒif ich der seggen [if I dare say it], mi leoue leafdi, þu ert min" (lines 157–158). In giving himself wholly to, and thus identifying himself with, Mary, he symbolizes his devotion to the life of wisdom, to being renewed in the spirit of his mind, to the rebirth which his spiritual state demands. He earlier has asked Mary as mother-physician to wash and clothe him (line 139); now he asks to behold Mary in heaven (line 165). Here again, Mary is not totally separate from her symbolic value, for to see Mary in heaven is to gain the bliss of heaven, the reward of a life of devotion to the spiritual values she embodies. In this way Mary may be said to represent the spiritual ideal much as the courtly beloved represented an ethical ideal. If Dante spiritualized Beatrice, the Fathers had spiritualized Mary before him (as Christ had done before them in a different sense in Mary's Assumption). If clerkly poets present Mary in terms appropriate to the courtly beloved, it is because the courtly relationship is analogous to the spiritual one. But, as with all analogies, it has limitations. As Hilary of Poitiers advises in another connection, "There can be no comparison between God and earthly things. . . . We must therefore regard any comparison as helpful to man rather than descriptive of God." [9] If the clerkly poets overemphasize their devotion to Mary in earthly terms, they have yielded to the weaknesses of the analogy between corporeal and spiritual.

This ecclesiastical Marian tradition of which we have been speaking flourished in the Middle Ages long before the development of courtly love, and spiritual writers praised Mary's great beauty, her sweetness, her role as lady and the servitude of her followers, her mercy, and her medicine to sinners at least as far back as the fourth century and the first great Marian doctor, St. Ephraem of Syria (whose influence, incidentally, spread from Spain to Ireland to seventh-century England).[10] We find these motifs in the seventh century in the Akathistos Hymn, Ildephonsus of Toledo, the Gothic and Mozarabic liturgies; in the eighth and ninth centuries in St. John Damascene, Alcuin, Ambrose Autpert, and the author of the *Epistola ad Paulam et Eustochium* (attributed to Jerome in the Middle Ages, but identified by modern scholars as Paschasius Radbert). In the tenth century we find them in the Little Office of the Blessed Virgin; in the eleventh in St. Peter Damian and St. Anselm of Canterbury. Only then do we find them in St. Bernard. And during the course of this tradition Mary is identified with *Sophia,* with *anima,* with *Ecclesia* through patristic exegesis and through liturgical use of the Song of Songs and the sapiential books. And the analogies which were drawn were more than mere pious fiction, for they derived from the actual, historical Mary who bore the Savior of the World.

The strong ecclesiastical tradition enabled the Middle English poet to draw freely from the similar courtly tradition. He did not always succeed in fusing the two traditions. How successfully he did fuse them, not that they were fused, should be the concern of the reader-critic. As I have already complained, scholars in the past have badly overestimated, as well as misunderstood, the debt to the courtly tradition. To see for ourselves what sort of use the Middle English poets made of the courtly analogy, we shall examine "Nou skrinkeþ rose ant lylie flour" (Brook, No. 23; XIV, No. 10) and "Edi beo þu, heuene quene" (XIII, No. 60). Neither poem shows any great French influence. In the latter poem, for example,

I find at most nineteen lines representing the secular tradition, but forty-five expressing the religious.* Strange statistics indeed if we accept Patterson's view that the poem illustrates "how intimately this spirit of the French secular songs had entered the English religious lyric" (p. 34). Apparently forgetting the liturgical sources he lists in his notes, he observes:

> The English poet, then, in uttering his cries for mercy has not prostrated himself before Mary of the liturgy, "most pitieous of alle pitieous wymmen"; nor is he altogether orthodox, one is forced to believe, for in his prayer he utters no irresistible plea for effective intermediation; he seems to have overlooked Mary's peculiar office. It is a return of affection for which he longs, while in his heart lie the pleading words of another nameless poet, "Yif me þi loue, ic am redi." So the attitude of the lady of the French songs, always marked by dignity, aloofness, and a certain *hauteur,* is assumed by the English poet to be characteristic of Mary. . . . (p. 35)

How convincingly this would demonstrate the influence of the French secular lyric if the poem itself did not contradict such a view! Lines 29–31 point out Mary's role in the salvation of mankind, which strikes me as more typical of the liturgy than Patterson's quotation. The lines read as follows:

> þu bring us ut of kare of drede
> þat Eue bitterliche us breuȝ,   *brewed*
> þu sschalt us in-to heouene lede.

There is no "irresistible plea" here, it is true—because the speaker makes his statement with absolute confidence.

---

* Secular: lines 5–8, 13–16, 22–24, 35–36, 45–48, 61–62; religious: lines 1–4, 9–12, 17–21, 25–34, 37–44, 49–60, 63–64. Since the traditions do overlap, distinguishing them seems more an academic pastime than anything else; but such statistics do help deflate exaggerated critical claims.

Lines 37–40 certainly reveal the speaker's awareness of "Mary's peculiar office," and the final two lines of the poem reveal the same thing:

> Þu me sschildȝe from þe feonde,
> ase þu ert freo & wilt & maucht,
> help me to mi liues ende,
> 40 & make me wið þin sone
>   isauȝt. . . .   *reconciled*

> leuedi, bring us to þine bolde,   *dwelling*
> 64 & sschild us from helle wrake.   *suffering*
>   AmeN.

Despite the strong religious tradition, the poet undoubtedly intends that we perceive some courtly analogies, for, like his contemporary, he sings of one who is matchless (XIII, No. 31). Four times he states his theme: lines 4, 13, 44, 61–62. Mary has no peer because she alone is the virgin-Mother of the Redeemer (line 6), but the poet extends her peerlessness. Not only by spiritual but even by worldly standards, Mary is completely matchless. The last stanza summarizes this quality:

> Þo godes sune aliȝte wolde   *when*
> on eorþe al for ure sake,
> herre teȝen he him   *He was not minded*
>   nolde   *to tie Himself higher*
> 60 þene þat mailde to beon his   *be*
>   make.   *mate*
> Betere ne miȝte he, þaiȝ he   *though*
>   wolde,
> ne swetture þing on eorþe take.

Herre has an ambivalence which points up exactly the implications of the thought: Christ was not minded to choose higher than an earthly woman to be His spouse, and yet could not have chosen a woman on earth higher in every quality than Mary. (The second meaning is made explicit in lines 61–62.) Therefore, when the speaker attributes to Mary certain qualities we associate with the courtly tradition, or uses the courtly analogy to describe his relationship to Mary, we must recognize that he is indicating Mary's superiority by worldly stand-ards. Mary, after all, comes from noble kin, of the house of David (lines 41–42). How appropriate, then, that the speaker think of her in courtly terms! Moreover, the relationship between the speaker and Mary resembles as much that between vassal and lady as lover and be-loved. In stanza five the speaker praises Mary's virtues and declares himself in her love-bonds (lines 33–36). But then he asks her for protection from the fiend, help to the end of his life, and reconciliation with Jesus (lines 37–40). Is this a request for "a return of affection"? Is this the tone of the troubadour? Some of the troubadour's conventions are here, certainly; the poet insists upon Mary's excellence in both the spiritual and earthly spheres. Because he does insist, he can unite the two traditions harmoniously.

Our second poem exhibits a different kind of French influence; indeed, some commentators may choose to refer it only to the ecclesiastical tradition. But even though it employs conventions which had been early assimilated into religious poetry, its allusions to the *pastourelle* create a background which heightens the thematic coloring.

> Nou skrinkeþ rose ant lylie-
>   flour
> þat whilen ber þat suete   *formerly bore*
>   sauour   *scent*
>   in somer, þat suete tyde;
> 4   ne is no quene so stark ne stour   *mighty   strong*
>   ne no leuedy so bryht in bour
>   þat ded ne shal by glyde.   *death   overtake*
>   Whose wol fleysh lust forgon   *whoever will forgo*

8 ant heuene blis abyde,   *expect*
  on Iesu be is þoht anon,
   þat þerled was ys side.   *pierced His*

  From Petresbourh in o morewe- *one morning*
   nyng,
12 as y me wende o my pleyȝyng, *pleasure*
   on mi folie y þohte; *illicit love thought*
  menen y gon my   *I began to utter my*
   mournyng   *grief*
  to hire þat ber þe heuene kyng,
16 of merci hire bysohte.   *implored*
  Ledy, preye þi sone for ous,
   þat vs duere bohte,   *dearly*
  ant shild vs from þe loþe hous *hateful*
20 þat to þe fend is wrohte.

  Myn herte of dedes wes fordred, *deeds frightened*
  of synne þat y haue my fleish
   fed
  ant folewed al my tyme,
24 þat y not whider i shal be led
  when y lygge on deþes bed, *lie*
   in ioie ore into pyne. *joy or into pain*
  On o ledy myn hope is,
28 moder ant virgyne,
  we shulen into heuene blis
   þurh hire medicine.

  Betere is hire medycyn
32 þen eny mede or eny wyn; *mead wine*
   hire erbes smulleþ suete; *sweet*
  from Catenas into Dyuelyn *Caithness to Dublin*
  nis þer no leche so fyn *physician*
36 oure serewes to bete. *assuage*
  Mon þat feleþ eni sor
   ant his folie wol lete, *abandon*

wiþoute gold oþer eny tresor
40   he mai be sound ant sete.   *content*

Of penaunce is his plastre al,   *her remedy*
ant euer seruen hire y shal
nou ant al my lyue;
44   nou is fre þat er wes   *who formerly was*
          þral,   *a slave*
al þourh þat leuedy gent ant   *through*
          smal;
heried be hyr ioies fyuel   *praised*
Wherso eny sek ys,   *wherever   sick*
48   þider hye blyue;   *thither let him hasten quickly*
þurh hire beoþ ybroht to blis   *are*
bo mayden ant wyue.   *both   wife*

For he þat dude is body on tre   *placed His*
52   of oure sunnes haue piete
þat weldes heouene boures!   *who governs*
Wymmon, wiþ þi iolyfte,   *gaiety*
þou þench on Godes shoures. *think on   pains*
56   þah þou be whyt ant bryht on   *in*
          ble,   *complexion*
falewen shule þy floures.   *fade*
Iesu, haue merci of me,
þat al þis world honoures.

In the opening stanzas, our poet utilizes five conventions
of French poetry, but to my knowledge the only single
French form in which they all appear is the *pastourelle*.[11]
These conventions are as follows: it is morning; the locale
is specifically mentioned; the speaker is alone; he goes
on his way "o my pleyȝyng" (the English equivalent of
the French *juer*); he is pensive—thinking, of course, of
love. Moreover, the rime scheme and metrical pattern
may also have been suggested by the *pastourelle*. William
P. Jones has observed that the *pastourelle* underwent a

great deal of experimentation in line lengths and rime schemes, so the few irregular lines and the shortened final stanza in our poem may reflect this experimentation.[12]

Our poet, however, takes the content of the *pastourelle*, in which the speaker wants the shepherdess to satisfy his lust, and reverses the whole idea:

> whose wol fleysh lust forgon
> 8   ant heuene blis abyde,
> on Iesu be is þoht anon,
> þat þerled was ys side.

Instead of writing a poem about a man who wanders by himself one fine spring morning and whose thoughts turn to love—or lust, as the poet prefers—he writes about what that man should have been thinking of in the first place —not fleshly desire, but Jesus Christ and his own salvation. The poet has viewed the *pastourelle* in terms of *de contemptu mundi:*

> 4   ne is no quene so stark ne stour,
> ne no leuedy so bryht in bour
> þat ded ne shal by glyde.

In this poem the speaker directs his advice toward both the participants of the *pastourelle*. He directs it toward the man who seeks to satisfy his lust by the example which he gives of himself; he is not thinking of lechery, but of his sins. He directs it toward the girl who would consent by three explicit references: lines 4–6, 49–50, 54–57. The *pastourelle*, then, is the background against which our poet paints his *contemptus mundi*.

Apart from the courtly analogies which accompany our poet's reversal of the *pastourelle*, a second use of analogy underlies the poem's structure. The transitoriness of earthly things is the lesson of nature herself, as the poet tells us at the very beginning (lines 1–3). He then expands this reflection to include human nature (lines 4–6). But thoughts of decay on the natural level

lead easily to decay on a supernatural level. The first six
lines not only set the mood of the poem and introduce
the basic image of decay, but they serve also as contrast.
Unlike the inevitability of natural decay, supernatural
decay is caused by man himself, and he has within his
own power the means of remedy: "whose wol fleysh lust
forgon . . . on Iesu be is þoht anon" (lines 7–9). Having
made this general observation, the speaker offers us a
personal application (stanza two). He thinks of his own
sins and directs his "mournyng" to the Virgin Mary,
asking her mercy. He then elaborates upon his supernatural condition, considering how he has fed his flesh
with sin (line 22, which recalls line 7). In this state of
spiritual sickness, the speaker then turns to Mary. (In
the background here is the popular pun on the Latin
salus, meaning both health and salvation.) The image of
medicine (line 30) not only continues the basic image of
decay but also reintroduces the theme of Christ's redemption of mankind: Christ is Mary's medicine (line 30),
thus emphasizing Mary's role in man's salvation. The
image of Mary as physician is developed in the fourth
and fifth stanzas; lines 39–40 have a particularly fine
allusion which shows that times have not changed: instead of the exorbitant fee one might expect, the only
payment necessary is forsaking our "folie." In order to
be cured, one ordinarily went to a "leche" (line 35) to
let blood; on a spiritual level one went to Mary to let
"folie" (line 38). The medicinal quality of penance (line
41) is traditional; [13] the image in the poem, however, is
precise and apt: just as a poultice draws soreness from
the body, so penance draws sins from the soul.

The final stanza accentuates the contrast between
natural and supernatural decay. It reminds us that all
earthly beauty fades (line 57), as the rose and lily in the
opening stanza (line 1). The speaker then addresses Jesus
directly for the first time (lines 58–59), for He died for
man's sins and, since He is Mary's medicine (line 31),

He will heal the speaker's supernatural sickness. Thus the speaker moves again from signs of natural decay to his spiritual state. Finally, the poet suggests that the natural decay of a woman's features brought about by the pains of childbirth (*shoures,* line 55) sent from God may indicate a simultaneous spiritual decay if the woman has, as the shepherdess, yielded to the man's lust. This poem, then, is a religious imitation of the *pastourelle* and owes certain conventions and possibly its rime scheme and metrical pattern to that genre. The poet has inverted the content of the *pastourelle* and colored it with *contemptus mundi.* His borrowings from the French, therefore, have a special significance, and the two traditions—religious and secular—blend harmoniously.

The analogy which the medieval poets saw between the natural and supernatural worlds is reflected in other poems. Few read the book of nature as carefully as the author of "Nou goth sonne vnder wod"; often they see in nature a warning for man of the transitoriness of life, but none expresses it so well as the author of "Wynter wakeneþ al my care" (XIV, No. 9; Brook, No. 17). The falling of the leaves reminds the speaker of how the joy of this world goes to nothing. In the final stanza the analogy is heightened:

> Al þat gren me graueþ   *All that greenery   grows*
>   grene; [14]   *green for me*
> 12   nou hit faleweþ al bydene—   *withers forthwith*
>   Ihesu, help þat hit be sene,
>   ant shild vs from helle,
>   for y not whider y shal ne
>   hou longe her duelle.

The speaker beholds in the flourishing and the fading of the trees a lesson for his own life; yet the cycle is brief, too brief perhaps for man to notice, and the speaker prays that Jesus help him perceive the lesson. He is concerned not only about where he will spend his eternity, but also, more immediately and fearfully important, about how much longer he will have in order to prepare himself for his eternity. Nature fades quickly; death comes suddenly. It is certain, yet it is uncertain. What is to prevent man from flourishing today and dying tomorrow? Autumn has driven home its spiritual significance. More complex interpretations of nature are generally reserved for application to Christ and Mary. Mary is the virgin soil in which God sows His seed, the flower upon which God showers the dew, the star that emits a ray of light. Most images of this type are either biblical or liturgical; too often they have become for the poets nothing more than stereotypes. The sense of wonder and exaltation that we find in St. Francis appears rarely. Sometimes the poets show familiarity with the bestiaries or the lapidaries, but their handling of these familiar images often makes us wish that they had used primary instead of secondary sources.

The analogies which the Middle Ages saw between the corporeal and the spiritual levels of existence is, as we have been noting, reflected in the imagery which the poets use. If we restrict imagery, as I do here, to include primarily simile, metaphor, allegory, and symbol, the poets wrote many image-less lyrics. And when we examine those that do contain imagery, we often find the images very few and insignificant in the structure of the poem as a whole. Why? Perhaps for three related reasons. First, the song and songlike lyric do not need imagery in this restricted sense to create their characteristic effects. Imagery, particularly metaphor and symbol, may bear too great an intellectual content for the songlike lyric. It suits better the insight into religious experience which these lyrics do not present. As we have observed, they tend rather to affirm the generally understood forms of religious experience. If they employ images, they find most helpful those which alliterate and those which are thoroughly conventional, for such images will not deflect attention from the sound pattern. Indeed the medievals valued imagery, not for its rich emotional overtones, but for its ability to stimulate the mind toward the supernatural. As D. W. Robertson has commented:

> the function of figurative expression was not to arouse spontaneous emotional attitudes based on the personal experience of the observer, but to encourage the observer to seek an abstract pattern of philosophical significance beneath the symbolic configuration.[15]

This leads to a second consideration. The Franciscans, who were so influential in shaping the course of the Middle English religious lyrics, were concerned more with arousing emotional response with their poems than they were in philosophical significances. There existed, in fact, a controversy between the friars and the secular clergy over the respective emphasis given devotional poetry and allegorical poetry.[16] Poetry written under Franciscan influence definitely did not tend to use imagery to illumine familiar religious concepts; unlike that poetry which used imagery to encourage the search for abstract philosophical patterning, its concerns were more to arouse spontaneous emotional attitudes.

A third reason, not so much for the lack of imagery but for the types of imagery used, issues from the didactic purpose of many of the lyrics and the confusion in general of rhetoric and poetic. Clarity—not ambiguity—is the chief aim of the rhetorician and the teacher. He is not primarily interested in a characteristic poetic technique of striking several notes at the same time. His images therefore tend to be single-dimensional. They clarify, but they do not illumine; they restrict, but they do not simultaneously expand. Rather than being intrinsic to the thought, they merely illustrate it. Once they have served their immediate purpose, they disappear. Indeed, because they are usually single-dimensional, they can encompass only a small portion of the theme and must be dropped. One poet, speaking of Christ on the cross, comments: "Als streme dose of þe strande [seashore], his blode gan downe glyde" (XIV, No. 83, line 40). This image focuses the abundance of the bleeding and is therefore more precise and carries a stronger emotive value than a less specific statement. But there is no insight. There is no suggestion of the infinite rivers of grace, of the "laver of redemption," of the spiritually cleansing power of Christ's blood. The image restricts but does not expand; it therefore remains single-dimensional. This characteristic sometimes rankles when the image appears over a number of lines and is then dropped. In three instances the image takes up half the poem, then vanishes: XIV, Nos. 62 and 63; XV, No. 68. But the poet has in all three instances developed the single dimension of the image about as far as it can go, and he must either invest it with added meanings or abandon it. The rhetorician generally prefers the latter. Even more suggestive of the rhetorician is the explicit exegesis with which he invests his image, especially when he uses allegory and feels obliged to make his point perfectly clear. (In fact, the single-dimension of many similes is reminiscent of the one-to-one equation of allegory.) But this quality is not confined to allegory; the following lines referring to Christ illustrate the technique at its baldest (XIV, No. 48):

Brother & syster he es by skyll,	*reason*
For he sayd & lered þare lare,	*taught*
Þat who-so wroght his fader will	*performed*
36	Brother & syster to him þai ware.	

Such a flat and obvious technique may contribute to the poet's realization of his theme as a whole, but it sorely limits his poem's ultimate literary worth.

Despite the influence of the song, of the Franciscans,

and of the rhetoricians and preachers, we can discover
some highly effective images in the religious lyrics. We
can even find multivalent images reminiscent of modern
use of symbolism. At this point we should recall the
historical use of analogy in the Middle Ages—that perspective which viewed the events of the New Testament
as reflected in the Old, as repeated in the life of the
Church, as exemplifying the life of every individual soul,
and as prophesying the life to come. The Middle Ages
often referred collectively to these levels of interpretation
as *allegory.* We would probably call it symbolism. The
medievals did, however, distinguish between what we
might term symbol and allegory; their terms were *allegoria in res* and *allegoria in verbis.* The primary basis
for this distinction lay in the treatment of the literal
level.[17] In *allegoria in verbis* the literal level has no real
significance; it is, as Dante calls it, "a beautiful lie." The
literal basis of *allegoria in res,* however, lies in actual
fact. This literal basis may be a thing (an eagle), a person
(Adam), or an event (the Israelites crossing the Red Sea).
In each instance the spiritual significance given the actual
object, person, or event derives from a Christocentric
view of the universe, an attempt to relate all things to
the Christian life. Thus, the exegetes detected an analogy (1) between the Old and New Testaments, applying
the signification to Christ either in His own life or in
the life of His Church; (2) between the corporeal and
spiritual worlds, in which the corporeal indicates a
course of supernatural action which the individual Chris-
tion should follow; and/or (3) between this temporal
existence, as reflected in actual history, and the life of the
world to come. Basically, then, this symbolism (as we call
it) works on two levels—a literal and a spiritual. The
spiritual level, in turn, is capable of interpretation on
three different planes, sometimes called respectively the
allegorical, the tropological, and the anagogical.[18] Perhaps a clearer set of terms is Christological-ecclesiological,

moral, and eschatological. We cannot insist too much on
the fact that each of these levels arises from the preceding.
What applies to Christ or the Church as a whole applies
as well to the individual soul, for Christ or the Church
is the model for the individual soul to copy. Similarly,
what characterizes the life of the soul on earth foreshadows its existence in heaven. And of course all these
spiritual interpretations are based on the literal fact.
Such an elaborate interrelationship of values is thus not
only meaningful, but coherent and unified as well. The
same image may not yield all three spiritual interpretations, however; the value may fluctuate from context
to context. Moreover, the particular significance which
the object yields may also vary: the eagle, for example,
may symbolize St. John, or Christ, or mankind—but these
interpretations are not necessarily mutually exclusive.
Sometimes the same object may embody opposite values:
the lion may be either Christ or the devil, and both these
significations may be traced to scriptural bases (Rev.
v.5 and 1 Pet. v.8). We must not forget that the symbolic
value which the Middle Ages saw in the things of this
world gave those things their worth; nature was valuable
for the Christian because it reflected God, the supreme
reality. As Otto von Simson has pointed out, in differen-
tiating medieval from modern times,

> For us the symbol is an image that invests physical
> reality with poetical meaning. For medieval man,
> the physical world as we understand it has no reality
> except as a symbol. But even the term "symbol" is
> misleading. For us the symbol is the subjective crea-
> tion of poetic fancy; for medieval man what we
> would call symbol is the only objectively valid
> definition of reality. We find it necessary to suppress
> the symbolic instinct if we seek to understand the
> world as it is rather than as it seems. Medieval man
> conceived the symbolic instinct as the only reliable
> guide to such an understanding.[19]

Since we are thus accustomed to taking the word *symbol* as representing a poetic rather than a metaphysical reality, and since a religious symbol may or may not function as a poetic symbol, I think that for our present purposes in trying to determine the literary quality of the religious lyrics, we should maintain the usual modern distinction between allegory and symbol, and use the threefold spiritual analogy as possible connotations of either.

Allegory may be defined, according to Robin Skelton, as "an image having apparent independence within a poem, but being, in reality, dependent upon an explicit identification of it with a concept or idea." A symbol, on the other hand, is "An image, possessing great associative value, and multiplicity of meanings, which acts independently within the poem, and is not dependent upon any comparison with, or equation with, a concept or idea." [20] In other words, allegory *tends* to give a one-to-one equivalence to the image (vehicle) and the idea or person to whom it refers (tenor); symbol is generally multivalent, or at least bivalent. In allegory the image exists for the sake of the idea; it in effect substitutes for it. In symbol the image exists first as a literal, concrete object and then suggests some abstract principle(s). Varieties are possible within each classification, and Skelton has listed and named these possibilities. To avoid so much nomenclature, however, we shall simply note relevant branches without giving them specific names.

The following image clearly illustrates what a symbol is not: "The pasche lambe, þat on þe croce did clym" (XV, No. 112, line 23). Now lambs—paschal or otherwise—do not ordinarily climb crosses. The literal meaning of this line is nonsense, and therefore does not contain a poetic symbol. Even though the paschal lamb is one of the most widespread religious symbols of Christ, it does not function here independently of its tenor and is therefore not a poetic symbol. It is instead a species of

allegory—even though it has multiple connotations. This
particular kind of allegory I will give a specific name,
for it is a device occasionally found in rhetoric. It is a
figurative epithet without the noun it describes; the
epithet appears in place of the noun. In this sense it is
a kind of synecdoche since one term (the epithet) is
used in place of another (the noun described). The technical name is antonomasia, but I shall call it simply
figurative epithet. This same device turns up in such
literally impossible lines as "When aungels brede [bread,
i.e., Christ] was dampned to dede to safe oure sauls sare"
(XIV, No. 83, line 44); "And seyde che [Mary] xuld
[should] bere the flour / That xulde breke the fyndes
[fiend's] bond" (Greene, No. 175C, lines 7–8); "Thow
[Mary] art the sterre with brestis softe as sylke" (XV,
No. 135, line 8). Each of these images has multiple connotations, but is not a poetic symbol simply because it
is literally impossible. If, as in these instances, the image
is conventional enough and appears only in passing, the
poet can substitute such epithets for the persons without
unduly upsetting his audience. And if he employs them
in a conspicuous sound pattern, he is even less likely to
disturb them.

The poet's failure to keep in mind the literal value
of the image can become disturbing in allegory, however,
for here the image has been developed, and the modern
mind seizes upon the discrepancy. The first stanza of a
sixteenth-century carol (Greene, No. 321) offers a familiar
allegorical interpretation of John xii. 24–25:

> On Cristes day, I vnderstond,
> An ere of whet of a mayd
>   spronge,
> Thirti winter in erth to stond,
> 4   To make vs bred all to his pay.   *liking*

The image is allegory, not symbol, for ears of wheat do
not spring from maidens. But watch what happens in
stanza two:

This corn was repyn and layd to growynd
Full sore beten and faste bownd
Vnto a piler with cordes rownd;
8   At his fyngers endes the blod ran owt that
          day.

Tenor and vehicle have become so identified in the poet's mind that he does not observe the properties of the vehicle as it actually exists. No wonder that the vehicle disappears completely from the last stanza! Although the sound pattern helps cover the flaw, we still object because the image extends beyond reason. We do not object because we cannot *visualize* a grain of wheat being scourged, but because the comparison between the reaped grain and the scourged Christ includes details (lines 7–8) appropriate to the latter but not to the former. Now observe line 2; here the discrepancy is not quite as glaring since *spronge* continues the image and since the thought is passed over quickly. The second stanza, though, points up the artificiality of the allegory: it is ornamental here rather than functional.

Allegory may thus be divided into two types: arbitrary and descriptive.[21] Arbitrary allegory is self-explanatory; the vehicle bears no relationship whatever to the tenor. For example, in "Ful feir flour is þe lilie" (XIII, No. 19), the vehicle is the lily which has five leaves, interpreted as charity toward God; love of neighbor; righteousness; then

      to seruen crist vid feid &   *with feet*
         honden,
      to firsaken tricherie,
24   prude & onde & lecherie;   *envy*

and finally, confession. This interpretation of the five leaves of the lily does nothing to elucidate the nature of the lily, nor on the other hand, does the nature of the five leaves of the lily have anything to do with the fivefold significance. Why not a lily with four leaves? The relation between image and signification is, in other words, purely arbitrary. The signification could be any other signification as long as it consists of five points; the choice of image could have been any image which suited a fivefold interpretation.

On the other hand, descriptive allegory contains some sort of intrinsic likeness between vehicle and tenor; it consequently exhibits some kind of interaction which makes possible an incisive comparison of tenor and vehicle. Descriptive allegory, therefore, can, at its best, penetrate directly into the theme. The poems which speak of Mary as rose are descriptive allegories, and usually they make explicit the similarities which make the comparison appropriate: beauty, excellence, love, virginity (usually when without thorns). But one of the most striking instances of this type of allegory is the opening of "Somer is comen & winter gon" (XIII, No. 54). After introducing the joyousness of spring, with the song of the birds, the poet continues:

	So stronge kare me bint,	*binds*
	al wit Ioye þat is funde	
	in londe,	
8	Al for a child	
	þat is so milde	
	of honde.	

	Þat child, þat is so milde & wlong		*proud*
12	& eke of grete munde,		*power*
	boþe in boskes & in bank		*bushes*
	isout me hauet a-stunde.	*sought*	*for a time*
	Ifunde he heuede me,		
16	for an appel of a tre		
	ibunde;		
	He brac þe bond		
	þat was so strong		
20	wit wunde.		

Þat child þat was so wilde &   *accustomed to*
     wlong   *taking His own way*
   to me a-lute lowe,   *bowed*
  fram me to giwes he was sold—   *Jews*
24   ne cuþen hey him nout   *They could not*
    cnowe.   *know Him*

Child here is obviously Christ, but the image is ambiva-
lent. In one sense Jesus is a youth of noble birth, "milde
/ of honde" (lines 9–10), yet proud as befits his nobility,
and of great power (lines 11–12). His power is shown,
in fact, by His breaking the strong bond of sin by His
wounds. The speaker, now Everyman, re-emphasizes that
this noble youth is proud and accustomed to taking His
own way (line 21); this prepares for the contrast in the
following line, recalling Phil. ii.8. But *child* also has
connotations here of regained youth, of regeneration,
so that the image thereupon assumes definite associations
with the springtime of the Redemption, the time of
rebirth and renewal. Finally, that Jesus is a youth sold
to the Jews reminds us of a favorite exegesis of the Old
Testament story of Joseph. What makes the image so
striking are these multiple connotations; the poet is
emphasizing his insight into the nature of the redemptive
act through the image of the child. Although the rest
of the poem has many excellent touches, including a
brilliant handling of variation in the sound pattern, I
do not feel that it matches this opening section.

That allegorical images can have multiple connotations is, I hope, sufficiently obvious. If there is any doubt,
this splendid carol should dispel it (Greene, No. 322A):

Lully, lulley; lully, lulley;
The fawcon hath born my mak away.

He bare hym vp, he bare hym down;
He bare hym into an orchard brown.

In that orchard ther was an hall,
4   That was hangid with purpill and pall.

And in that hall ther was a bede;
Hit was hangid with gold so rede.

And yn that bed ther lythe a knyght,
8   His wowndes bledyng day and nyght.

By that bedes side ther kneleth a may,
And she wepeth both nyght and day.

And by that beddes side ther stondith a ston,
12   *Corpus Christi* wretyn theron.

Lines 11–12 clearly mark this poem as allegory: the knight is Christ, Mary or Ecclesia is the *may*. We have a definite one-to-one relation. Moreover, lines 1–2 undoubtedly allude to the garden where the sepulchre was (John xix.41), with a possible further allusion to the apple tree in Eden. Now the connotations here are multiple. The poem is reminiscent of a typical ballad situation, but even more so of the Grail Legend and the myth of the dying God. (This connotation marks the poem even more strongly as allegory.) Finally, there are suggestions of the Eucharistic host and possibly a remote connection with the Mass.[22] The situation, in fact, calls to mind the Forty Hours Devotion, which commemorates the forty hours Christ spent in the tomb. During this time the Blessed Sacrament is exposed on the altar for the adoration of the faithful. This devotion, in fact, dates from the sixteenth century, the date Greene gives the MS of our poem.[23] Perhaps this poem was written in celebration of, or was inspired by, the devotion. The hall may well be the physical church; the bed, the monstrance; the may, Ecclesia; the stone, the altar stone upon which the monstrance rests. The continuous bleeding supports the Catholic dogma of the Real Presence. The stone also contributes something to this doctrine; it is traditionally a symbol of rebirth and clearly refers to the stone over the tomb which the holy women found rolled away on Easter morning. The image thus emphasizes the reality of Christ's existence and His divinity (since the Resurrection is considered the ultimate proof of His divinity). At any rate, the poem has nothing to do with Joseph of Arimathea, despite Annie Gilchrist's pleas and Greene's approval.[24]

The quality of this carol is, as Speirs has pointed out, a "strangely exciting" one: "One is led by steps as through a maze until one reaches the centre of the maze, the heart of the mystery." [25] The chief problem which the lyric poses is that of the refrain. Is it mere nonsense, equivalent ultimately to "Hey, nonny no"? Or does the refrain have a definite thought relationship to the rest of the poem? I prefer the latter solution since I feel that the poem is too artfully constructed to have a nonsensical refrain. Moreover, the *he* and *hym* of line 1 refer to the falcon and the mate in the refrain, so the refrain surely must have a meaning. The first thing we have to determine is the tenor of each vehicle in the refrain. "My mak" is obviously Christ; the falcon is probably death. The second thing to determine is the speaker. It may be the *may* of line 10, for the familiar lullaby suggests Mary and her Child. Or it may be Ecclesia paradoxically soothing her children, for Christ's death has once more established peace between God and man and can occasion the sense of calm and well-being connoted by the first line of the refrain. Moreover, Ecclesia daily remembers the sacrifice of Calvary through the sacrifice of the Mass. If Mary speaks the refrain, the emotional intensity of the poem increases; if Ecclesia, the poet shows a greater insight into the significance of the Crucifixion. I prefer the latter.

The Corpus Christi carol is, as we have seen, allegory

because the knight is not a knight, but Christ. Because of the last couplet, the image does not exist independently of its signification. A symbolic image does, and this is the basic distinction between the two kinds of image. Symbols are rare in the religious lyric, and I shall illustrate them by Herebert's English translation of the "Hostis Herodis impie" (XIV, No. 12):

> Herodes, þou wykked fo,
>   whar-of ys þy dredinge?
> And why art þou so sore agast
>   of cristes to-cominge?
> Ne reueth he nouth erthlich   *robs*
>   god þat maketh ous heuene   *good*
>   kynges.

> 4   Þe kynges wenden here way
>   and foleweden þe sterre,
> And sothfast lyȝth wyth sterre-
>   lyth souhten vrom so   *sought from*
>   verre,   *far*
> And sheuden wel þat he ys god   *showed*
>   in gold and stor and   *incense*
>   mirre.

> Crist, y-cleped heuene lomb, so   *called*
>   com to seynt Ion
> 8   And of hym was y-wasȝe þat   *washed*
>   sunne nadde non,   *sin had*
> To halewen our vollouth *sanctify baptismal*
>   water þat sunne hauet
>   uordon.   *destroyed*

> A newe myhte he cudde þer he   *showed*
>   was at a feste: *feast*
> He made vulle wyth shyr *made to be filled clear*
>   water six cannes by þe
>   leste,

12   Bote þe water turnde in-to wyn
    þorou crystes oune heste.   *command*

  Wele, Louerd, boe myd þe, þat   *glory*
    shewedest þe to-day
  Wyth þe uader and þe holy gost
    wythouten ende-day.   *ending*

On the literal level this poem speaks of the threefold manifestation (epiphany) of Christ as God. The first stanza announces the coming of God to earth and establishes Him as a spiritual monarch. Each of the next three stanzas presents one of these manifestations of Christ as God: to the Magi, to the Jews at His baptism (Mark i.9–11), and to the Apostles at the marriage at Cana (John ii.1–11). The final stanza translates the doxology and refers to the theme of manifestation. The Latin hymn appears in the Divine Office for the feast of the Epiphany, which originally commemorated the other two events as well before they were transferred to the Sundays succeeding the Epiphany. The liturgy, in fact, contains the key to the symbolic value. Each of these events has a spiritual significance in addition to its role in the threefold manifestation of Christ as God. We have a basis for the symbolic interpretation in line 3 with the reference to Christ's making us kings of heaven. The word *kings,* in fact, ties the symbolic significance to the first event: the kings (Magi) were symbols of the Gentiles, and their worship of the Child represents the calling of the Gentiles. The second event, Christ's baptism, symbolizes our own, by which we are entitled to enter heaven. The third event, the changing of water into wine, symbolizes our own transformation from a purely human nature into partakers of the divine nature through sanctifying grace and thus truly making us kings of heaven. Thus the two themes—Christ's manifestation of His divinity and our calling to and participation in His divine nature—are

closely interwoven. Yet the literal theme exists independently of the symbolic (but not vice versa); it is
this, in fact, which marks the poem as symbolic rather
than allegorical. But are we justified in this symbolic
interpretation? I contend that we are, for patristic
exegeses and the liturgy itself suggest such a tropological
(or moral) interpretation. If Herebert knew the liturgical
original of his poem, why would he not have known its
symbolic interpretation as well? [26]

In examining the relationship between a poet's use
of imagery and his religious subject matter, we can
easily see that to be effective, arbitrary allegory depends
upon an imaginative intensity, since it offers little insight
into its subject. Descriptive allegory, on the other hand,
can, along with symbol, illumine the audience's generally
accepted notions. But since the poet relies by and large
on stock images, he runs the risk of depending upon the
inherent value of the imagery to illumine, rather than
modifying or extending this inherent value to suit his
context. He may, in effect, handle his imagery the way
he handles his formula of address plus petition—mechanically or organically. And if he handles it organically,
he may either increase the emotional intensity with
which the subject matter is usually held, or may actually
penetrate the significance of his subject. The literary
quality, of course, lies in direct ratio to this presentation
of the subject matter.

Another aspect of the literary quality depends upon
the structural use to which a poet puts his images, and
in the lyrics we can detect two common structural patterns. Sometimes a poet may use multiple images, which
complement or even contradict one another; sometimes
he may use a basic image with multiple connotations,
around which the poem moves concentrically. The former
technique is often accompanied by parallelism and occasionally shows linear structure. Ordinarily the Middle
English religious poets handle this technique most ef-

fectively when the poem is short and exemplifies thematic evolution, as in the following:

He yaf himself as good felowe,		*gave*
Whan he was boren in wre		*born*
wede;		*clothing*
Als good norice he bowh	*as nurse*	*bowed*
down lowe,		
4 Whan wiht himself he wolde		*with*
us fede.		*feed*
Als good schephirde upon ȝe		*the*
lowe,		*hill*
His wed he yaf for wre nede;		*gave*
In hevene as king we schulen		
him knowe,		
8 Qwan he himself schal yiven		
in mede.[27]		

Each of the four images represents some aspect of Christ's
love for mankind; they are presented in chronological
order, referring to the Incarnation, the institution of the
Holy Eucharist, the Crucifixion, and the union of the
individual soul with Christ after death. The first image
is striking; *good felowe* suggests the tone of our modern
"regular guy." This colloquial tone is not at all ir-
reverent, for it underscores the tremendous humility
manifested by the Incarnation. The image of the nurse
very aptly expresses Christ's giving Himself in the
Eucharist; bowing down low recalls Phil. ii.8 and refers
to the Incarnation as well as to the literal image of feeding. The third image reminds us that the Good Shep-
herd lays down His life for His sheep (John x.15), and
the poet puns upon the hill of Calvary. The last two
lines carry definite sexual connotations, suggesting something like mystical union. Now although the poet has
chosen four vigorous independent images, he has also
interlinked them effectively. The clothing image joins
lines 2 and 6 with a paradoxical twist: Christ assumed

our garment so that He might give it up for our neediness. The concept of Christ's giving Himself to us joins lines 4 and 8. In the former it is as food in Holy Communion; in the latter it is as lover in final union. The juxtaposition of these two thoughts relates them notionally, and the poet seems to establish the first as a foretaste of the second. In addition to the chronological order and the interlinking of images, the poet unifies his work by the thought of the last two lines, which climax the thought structure. He has been speaking of Christ as man, but in heaven we will recognize Christ for what He is—God as well as man. This thought completes the familiar circular pattern begun in lines 1–2: God descended to become man in order that He might raise man up to Him. Admittedly, this is a minor poem, but the poet has fashioned his materials with considerable skill.

Perhaps the poem which comes closest to handling the multiple-image technique the way modern readers know it is Thomas of Hales' love ron (XIII, No. 43). The poem divides readily into halves, and its images reflect a general thematic content of nature vs. grace. The introduction sets up the *raison d'être* for the poem; the good Friar seems to be enjoying a little joke. Apparently some young lady who dedicated herself to God's service (in a general sense) requested Friar Thomas to compose for her a poem containing advice on taking a second true lover (other than God, presumably). Having thus set up the circumstances, the text proceeds with the ron. In the first part (lines 9–88) the speaker contemplates the transitoriness of this world with its joys and gifts. Trust in such ephemeral love, he warns, and you place your trust wrongfully. Moreover, a true lover cannot be found in this world; truth in love lasts forever, not just until death, and this world is by nature transitory. Therefore in the second part (lines 89–192) the speaker describes, as the young lady wished, the truest and best man. But there is no "other" man involved—it is Christ Himself Whom the speaker describes. He emphasizes in this section the virtue of chastity, a treasure consigned by Christ, so that, paradoxically, by remaining chaste the girl may have a Lover Who will remain true forever. This motif of virginity is accented by the allusion in the closing lines to the Annunciation scene (lines 205–206). The theme of the inevitability of natural decay is, as we have said, the dominant theme of the first part of the poem. The author draws six images from nature to describe the lot of the earthly lover and all his attributes, and the characteristics of the world itself: the lover glides away as does a blast of wind (line 14); he fades as meadow grass (line 16); this world is as the shadow that glides away (line 32); it is as wind (line 39); [28] the lover will wither as the leaf on the bough (line 48); he has glided out of the kingdom as the blade cuts off the head from the sheaf (lines 71–72).[29] The fact that these multiple images are drawn from nature underscores the fact that it is man's nature to die. (Most of these images also have biblical overtones, thus verifying the certainty of the comparisons.) Therefore, if we seek a true love who will remain true forever, we must seek elsewhere.

In the second part of the poem we find three other images drawn from nature, but this time the natural objects fall short of the object being compared. The girl herself, while she guards her castle, i.e., her body, is sweeter than any flower (lines 151–152) and sweeter than any spice (lines 167–168); the gem of her chastity is more precious than any other precious stones, including those of which heaven itself is constructed (lines 169–176).[30] The suggestion in these images is that the maiden of the poem is placing herself above a mere natural plane by remaining chaste, for she guards the treasure which Christ has consigned to her (line 145). Yet the fact that she will thus be (implicitly) a flower sweeter than any earthly flower, a spice sweeter than any earthly spice, and that her chastity itself is a gem more valuable than any earthly gem suggests that this is part of man's nature too. He has a soul which is immortal and therefore capable of true (i.e., eternal) love. To realize this capability, man must raise himself above the merely natural level through sanctifying grace, a gift which God freely bestows upon him (line 111) so that He may become the soul's lover. Only through this gift can man transcend his mortal nature and fulfill his potential supernaturally. Friar Thomas stresses this transcendence by presenting Christ as better than any mere earthly lover, for only He is capable of loving truly (i.e., forever). Our poet can now ask:

> Ne doþ he, mayde, on vuele dede   *a foul deed*
> þat may cheose of two þat on,
> & he wile wiþ-vte neode   *needlessly*
> 192   take þet wurse, þe betere let gon?

He has anticipated this argument in the first part by declaring that whoever places his love in this world acts as a blind man (lines 37–38); in other words he is deliberately depriving himself of what is properly his—his eyesight. Similarly, in this second part, man deprives his soul of what is properly hers—her one true Lover—if he chooses a worldly lover. These various image-groups, then, weigh the natural (mortal) against the supernatural (eternal), or nature and God's grace, just as their respective sections contrast the worldly and the spiritual. If a modern poet wrote this poem, he might have preferred to use symbol rather than allegory (he at any rate would not have felt it necessary to explain his allegory); so might have Friar Thomas, but he wanted above all to make his meaning clear (cf. lines 161–162) and preserve this maiden for Christ. If his purpose is consequently more rhetorical than poetic, he has nonetheless created an artistic whole—to which his use of multiple images skilfully contributes.

That medieval poets sometimes used imagery which is consistent and which approximates modern use must come as a surprise to those commentators who see little else but disjointedness in medieval literature in general. Moreover, we can even find effective use of a central image other than that afforded by allegory. "Vndo þi dore, my spuse dere" (XIV, No. 68), for example, makes the heart a central image which contains within itself the paradoxical theme of the poem. The poet has taken as his text Rev. iii.20; his treatment shows familiarity with the traditional glosses, but he manipulates his image independently of them. The poem opens by dramatizing the image: Christ, His hair dripping with blood, knocks at the locked door of the speaker's heart, beseeching entrance. (The situation recalls Songs v.2, and thus contributes heavily to the images of Christ as Lover and the soul as beloved.) Hearing Christ's plea, the speaker realizes that he has driven Him from his heart. He implores forgiveness, and resolves to open his heart to take in Christ, his true Love. In one sense, the poem is now over, but our poet adds six more lines of the speaker's reflections, which develop the basic image three ways:

For þin herte is clouen oure	*cleft*
loue to kecchen,	*catch*
Þi loue is chosen vs alle to	*has chosen*
fecchen;	*fetch*
Min herte it þerlede ȝef i were	*would pierce*
kende,	
20 Þi suete loue to hauen in	
mende.	
Perce myn herte with þi	
louengge,	
Þat in þe i haue my duellingge.	
Amen.	

The poet reserves the ultimate paradox of his image for the last line; in the meantime he introduces to the heart image the related image of the hunt or chase (*kecchen,*

fecchen), which restates the theme of the dramatized
opening lines. The heart now becomes the bait as well as
the prey. Second, these two meanings unfold more when
the speaker asks that his heart be cleft with the spear of
love, as Christ's was by Longinus' spear. The goal and
the bait again become synonymous as the speaker's heart
and Christ's become one. Finally, line 22 completes the
image by the paradoxical significance of the union of the
two meanings of the image; the speaker admits Christ to
the dwelling place of his heart in order that he may
thereby live in Christ. The union is so complete that they
dwell within each other simultaneously. The thought resembles that in John xv.4–5, although the image of the
heart seems less profound than that of the vine and
branches. Nonetheless, the poet's penetrating development of the image strongly suggests mystical union, and
he has achieved a complementary thematic and imagistic
unity.

On occasion the central image is much more complex than that of the heart, as in the following highly
praised and familiar instance (XIII, No. 17A):

> For ou [31] þat is so feir ant   *before you who are*
>   brist   *bright*
>   *uelud maris stella,*
> bristore þen þe dai-is list,   *day's*
> 4   *parens & puella,*
> i crie þe grace of þe:
> leuedi, prie þi sone for me,
>   *tam pia,*
> 8 þat i mote come to þe,
>   *maria.*
>
> Leuedi, best of alle þing,
>   *rosa sine spina,*
> 12 þou bere ihesu, heuene-king,
>   *gratia diuina.*

of alle þou berest þat pris,   *prize*
heie quen in parais
16   *electa:*
moder milde ant maiden ec
     efecta.

In car ant consail þou art best,
20   *felix fecundata;*
to alle weri þou art rest,
     mater honorata.
bi-hold tou him wid milde mod   *thou*
24   þat for us alle scedde is blod
     in cruce;
bidde we moten come to him
     in luce.

28   Al þe world it wes fur-lorn
     þoru *eua peccatrice*
to-forn þat ihesu was iborn
     ex te genitrice;
32   þorou *aue* e wende awei   *he turned aside*
     þe þestri nist, ant com þe dai   *the dark*
     salutis;
     þe welle springet out of þe
36   *uirtutis.*

Vuel þou wost he is þi sone   *well   know*
     uentre quem portasti;
he nul nout werne þe þi bone   *will not refuse*
40   *paruum quem lactasti.*
so god ant so mild e is,
he bringet us alle in-to is blis
     superni;
44   he hauet i-dut þe foule put   *shut   pit*
     inferni.

This poem is constructed upon two overlapping patterns:
first, an image pattern of light and darkness, and second,

a logic pattern, in no strict sense formal, and certainly naive, yet irrefutable in view of the strong religious faith which shapes it. This logic pattern, which reinforces and is reinforced by the image pattern, has two aspects: (1) what might be called argument from the general to the particular in the matter of Redemption, which involves a significant shift from *I* to *we;* (2) a pseudo-causal connection based upon the Mother-Son relationship. In the fourth stanza these two patterns unite and become clear. The image pattern is introduced in the opening line in *brist,* then modified by the traditional epithet *stella maris* (line 2). This simile connotes four things pertinent to the light pattern: grace, purity, a guiding light, begetter of Light. In fact, the usual interpretation of *stella maris* in the commentaries is twofold; Mary is so called first because she bore Christ (the basis of all her prerogatives) and then because she is guide to sinners.[32] The poet follows the usual order, devoting stanza two to her bearing Christ and stanza three to her role on behalf of mankind. A new connotation of the light image appears at the end of stanza three: heaven is light (line 27). In the fourth stanza the poet develops the fourth connotation of the light image: the birth of Christ brings the day of salvation (lines 33–34). Christ is, first of all, the Sun Whom the sea-star has brought forth.[33] Second, through Christ's birth the darkness of sin is turned away and the light of grace is brought to mankind. The light-dark pattern, then, centers on the Virgin as star of the sea, who illumines the darkness of this world and leads souls to herself (and her Son) in the light of heaven. She has these powers because she has brought forth the True Light and is thereby the light of grace in the day of salvation to the night of sin caused by Eve.[34] This rather elaborate, systematic interrelationship of images supports the logic pattern.

The speaker, then, has set up a basis for his request in Mary's role as star of the sea. He first asked for grace from Mary, who is herself full of grace and thereby "feir ant brist." In stanza two he reminds her that God gave her a special grace. Now in stanza four he reminds her that she has brought grace to all mankind. Since God has granted her so singular a grace as to become His mother yet retain her virginity, and since it was through her that grace in the form of redemption came to mankind, God will surely grant her the grace which the speaker requests. Further, since Mary brought the day of salvation to all mankind, surely she will bring it to that part of mankind for whom the speaker prays ("bidde *we* moten come to him," line 26). The poet sums up the fourth stanza with "þe welle springet out of þe /*uirtutis.*" The immediate meaning of this line lies in the contrast between sin and virtue, as in a contemporary Latin hymn: "Peccatum excluditur, / Virtus introducitur." [35] Another and more significant meaning does not emerge until the final stanza.

In the final stanza the shift in line 26 from *I* to *we* is clarified. Stanza four functions as an analogy with the request in stanza one. In the first stanza the speaker requests that Mary, by her light, lead him from the darkness of this world to the light of heaven. In stanza four he mentions an analogous situation: mankind in general was lost in the night of sin because of Eve, until Mary brought the day. The shift from *I* to *we,* then, is made in preparation for this generalization; the speaker uses a naive logic that, from a religious standpoint, possesses conviction. This logic works both independently of, and along with, the analogy developed in stanza four. First of all the poet reminds Mary that she is well aware Christ is her Son; if she is *maris stella* because she bore Christ, then surely she is *maris stella* as guide to sinners and will lead men to heaven by asking her Son for this grace. Christ, her Son, will not refuse her request, simply because He is her Son. The speaker, therefore, is confident that we shall all reach heaven (*bringet,* line 42, i.e., "will

bring"), and supports his confidence by reminding Mary
that Christ has shut up "þe foule put" (line 44) of hell.
This of course refers to the work of the Redemption, referred to as *day* in lines 33–34. *Foule put* and *inferni*
carry connotations of darkness, and implicit is another
analogy. Just as Mary brought day and turned away
night through the birth of Christ, so by the act of Redemption Christ delivered man from the darkness of
hell. Therefore He will surely deliver us from the darkness of this world, through the intercession of His Mother
—*stella maris*. And, by extended analogy, if He will deliver us, mankind, He will deliver me, the speaker. The
psychology of the generalization here suits the quasi-
logical approach of the poem.

In this poem, then, unlike many other lyrics, the shift
from *I* (line 8) to *we* (line 26) is significant. In one other
example the shift (although reversed) is significant:

we mowen iheren ant isen,	*that we may hear and see*
leuedi, for þi muchele miste,	*great power*
þe swete blisse of heuene briste,	
48 seinte marie, hernde me (XIII, No. 18).	*intercede for*

This speaker also argues from the general to the particular. Through Mary's might we are all entitled to heaven,
and the speaker claims his right, as it were, by requesting that Mary intercede for him and thus show her might
on a personal level. (*Miste* is an excellent synonym for
the idea in lines 35–36, as we shall see presently.) Our
poet, besides the meaningful shift from *I* to *we*, shifts
also from Mary (*þe*, line 8) to Christ (*him*, line 26). The
psychology involved here seems to be that Mary, the
mediatrix of all grace, is the special recourse of the individual; when Christ is spoken of, it is with less assurance
of personal salvation. In fact the entire argument is based

upon Mary's asking her Son for the grace the speaker requests, rather than approaching Christ directly.

The poem ends rather abruptly; from the point of view of the logic pattern, however, there is nothing more to say. But it is not strange that the poem concludes with attention focused on Christ, rather than Mary; the speaker does not even recapitulate nor make a final appeal to Mary. This shift in attention from Mary to Christ is complete, and this ties in with the poet's argumentative technique of approaching Christ through Mary. But Mary is not lost sight of in the last five lines. In the first place, the speaker still addresses her, reminding her of Christ's goodness. Second, we must now go back and reread lines 35–36. *Virtue* has the sense of "strength" or "power," and refers to Christ's stopping up the foul pit of hell and snatching mankind from the power of the devil. Mary, we recall, is the well from which this power has sprung (*springet*, historical present). But the present tense in line 35 can also have the sense of what we might call an "everlasting" present, and the relevance of this line depends upon its being read both as a historical present and as an ordinary present. It then becomes part of the logic pattern and rounds out the argument. If the power of God once sprang from Mary and the pit of hell was shut, then it will once again spring from Mary to keep the speaker from the darkness of hell. The reminder of Christ's achievement in lines 41–45, then, is also a reminder of Mary's participation, so that the poem concludes, not only with the image pattern, but also with the final argument in the logic pattern.*

"For ou þat is so feir ant brist" thus reflects the unity of existence which the medieval mind saw so acutely. The Incarnation has a personal meaning for the speaker; it is at the center of his own history, and the multiplicity

* This careful working out of the image and logic patterns distinguishes the Trinity version from the inferior Egerton MS.

of analogies which he summons to his support verifies his consciousness of the unity of existence. Similarly, the translation of the "Hostis Herodis impie" sees in the events of Christ's life a significance for His Church collectively and individually; His threefold epiphany symbolizes His marriage to *Ecclesia* and to *anima*. This interpretation comes direct from the liturgy, as indeed the hymn itself does. But the medievals saw other analogies not sanctioned by the liturgy; the Corpus Christi carol may have liturgical overtones, but its suggestions of the Grail myth and the dying God would automatically suggest to the Christian the ultimate reality behind all existence—God Himself. It is this attempt to pierce reality that the medieval use of imagery so clearly demonstrates. This world was very real for medieval man, but it would not last. It therefore could not be the ultimate reality. But this world was created by God, and God is reflected in His creation. Thus the medievals sought to perceive God—reality—in the natural world; thus the recipient of Thomas of Hales' love ron would respond immediately to the forcefulness of his use of natural images to support his theme of mutability. The fact that the medieval poet utilized traditional imagery did not mean that he was restricting the possibilities of what he could express. On the contrary, these images had a connotative richness simply because they did penetrate reality. Reality is multiple, is complex, indeed even contradictory. So also the imagery. But the ultimate reality is suprasensible, and imagery is sensible. Hence imagery can depict only fragments of that reality; hence one image must be modified by another. The danger inherent in traditional imagery for the medieval poet was not that it could express so little of his thought, but that he might rely on it too much in itself to express his thought. As with his subject matter and with forms borrowed from religious devotion, the poet could rely too much on the inherent value of his image. The best poets verify the truths inherent in their images or push the images even further into reality than they had been pushed before. "Wynter wakeneþ al my care" verifies emotionally the lesson of mutability; "Somer is comen & winter gon" places the image of the child in a context which invites multiple connotations in order to focus on the multiple spiritual significances of the Incarnation. Perhaps two questions come to mind in connection with the poets' use of imagery: Are we justified in reading all these connotations into medieval poetry? The applicability to biblical exegesis is perhaps clearer than it is to poetry explication. The second question is this: If these images are so complex, is this not attributing to the song a greater intellectual complexity than a song is able to bear? The answer to this question is our concern in the next chapter. The answer to the first question has been the subject of much dispute.[36] But a strong argument for the unity of existence seems necessarily to include an argument for poetic as well as biblical application. Why must we contend that the medieval clerk encountered patristic exegesis in the Divine Office, in the lessons read to him during meals in the monastery, in the books he copied; that he encountered it in the art and architecture of the church wherein he worshipped; that he used this same exegesis in his sermons, in his spiritual treatises, in his Latin hymns; but that when he sat down and wrote poetry in the vernacular, he completely divested himself of such folderol? His English poetry dealt with the same spiritual reality that those other forms dealt with—a reality so great that not even all the images in the world could express it. And yet these images have their purpose: "that by tho thinges that ben visible / and that man kyndely knoweth / he be stired and rauysched to loue and desire gostly invisible thinges that he kyndely knoweth not." [37]

1. *The Gothic Image,* trans. Dora Nussey (New York, 1958), p. 29. For other examples of the concept of the book of nature, see Henri de Lubac, *Exégèse médiévale* (Paris, 1959), I, 124; Curtius, pp. 319–326.

2. See Etienne Gilson, *La Philosophie de Saint Bonaventure,* Études de philosophie médiévale, IV (Paris, 1924), pp. 196–227.

3. See de Lubac, I, 305–328, 490–522.

4. "Le Symbolisme des rites baptismaux," *Dieu vivant,* I (1945), 17, as translated by Walter J. Burghardt, "On Early Christian Exegesis," *Theological Studies,* XI (1950), 79. See also Jean Daniélou, "Les Divers sens de l'Écriture dans la tradition chrétienne primitive," *Ephemerides theologicae Lovanienses,* XXIV (1948), 119–126.

5. *The Defence of Poesy,* in *Poetry of the English Renaissance,* ed. J. William Hebel and Hoyt H. Hudson (New York, 1929), p. 896.

6. E.g., see Rossell Hope Robbins, ed., *Secular Lyrics of the XIVth and XVth Centuries* (2nd ed.; Oxford, 1955), pp. li–liv.

7. See H. Coathalen, *Le parallelisme entre la Sainte Vierge et l'Église dans la Tradition latine jusqu'à la fin du XIIe siècle* (Rome, 1954); Victor White, "The Feminine Image in Christianity," *Soul and Psyche* (London, 1960), pp. 128–140. For the equation of Mary and Sophia in the liturgy, see esp. the Books of Hours.

8. *The Paradise Tree* (New York, 1959), p. 304.

9. *De Trinitate,* I, 19, quoted by Helen Flanders Dunbar, *Symbolism in Medieval Thought* (New Haven, 1929), p. 266.

10. F. J. E. Raby, *A History of Christian Latin Poetry* (2nd ed.; Oxford, 1953), p. 363; Edmund Bishop, "Liturgical Note," *The Book of Cerne,* ed. A. B. Kuypers (Cambridge, 1902), p. 280. For a survey of the Marian tradition, see Gabriel Roschini, *Mariologia* (Rome, 1947–48), II. For the imagery applied to Mary, see Anselm Salzer, *Die Sinnbilder und Beiworte Mariens* (Linz, 1893); Alfonso Rivera, "¿Sentido Mariológico del Cantar de los Cantares?" *Ephemerides Mariologicae,* II (1952), 25–42; Gabriel Roschini, "Royauté de Marie," in *Maria,* ed. Hubert du Manoir (Paris, 1952), I, 601–618.

11. The usual opening is in the spring, but some *pastourelles* do take place—as our poem—in autumn; e.g., Karl Bartsch, ed., *Altfranzösische Romanzen und Pastourellen* (Leipzig, 1870), Part II, Nos. 17 and 73. Moreover, this genre was sometimes moralized, as Jean Audiau remarks of several in his collection, *Le Pastourelle dans la poésie occitane du moyen-âge* (Paris, 1923), p. xiv. We also have examples of French religious poems which work within the *pastourelle* tradition; e.g., "A l'escuier mout grief estoit" and Gautier de Coinci, "Hui matin a l'ains jornei."

12. *The Pastourelle* (Cambridge, 1931), p. 4.

13. See John T. McNeill, "Medicine for Sin as Prescribed in

the Penitentials," *Church History*, I (1932), 14–26; *Medieval Handbooks of Penance* (New York, 1938), pp. 44–46.

14. An alternate reading which Brook accepts (p. 53) involves emending *gren* to *grein:* all that grain man buries unripe. Brown relates the thought to John xii.24–25 (XIV, p. 245), but the suggestion of decay in such a context seems more a cause for rejoicing than for melancholy. Furthermore, the image here moves away from that in stanza one. For other objections to the emended reading, see Edward Bliss Reed, "Wynter Wakeneth Al My Care," *MLN*, XLIII (1928), 81–84.

15. Ed., Saint Augustine, *On Christian Doctrine*, Library of Liberal Arts (New York, 1958), p. xv.

16. See Charles R. Dahlberg, "The Secular Tradition in Chaucer and Jean de Meun," unpublished dissertation (Princeton, 1953), esp. pp. 127–128. For the Franciscan influence on the English lyrics, see Rossell Hope Robbins, "The Authors of the Middle English Religious Lyrics," *JEGP*, XXXIX (1940), 230–238.

17. See Anthony Nemetz, "Literalness and the *Sensus Litteralis*," *Speculum*, XXXIV (1959), 76–89. For *allegoria in res* and *in verbis*, see de Lubac, I, 493–498. For Dante's distinctions, see Charles S. Singleton, "Dante's Allegory," *Speculum*, XXV (1950), 78–86; Richard Hamilton Green, "Dante's 'Allegory of Poets' and the Mediaeval Theory of Poetic Fiction," *CL*, IX (1957), 118–128.

18. De Lubac distinguishes a triple and a fourfold exegesis of Scripture (I, 139–157, 203), but this distinction is not necessary for our purposes. De Lubac also insists upon the importance of the literal level, pp. 425–439.

19. *The Gothic Cathedral*, Bollingen Series, XLVIII (New York, 1956), p. xix.

20. *The Poetic Pattern* (Berkeley, 1956), p. 102.

21. The terms are Helen Flanders Dunbar's; see esp. p. 476. I consider personification allegory more personification than allegory and do not discuss it. (It appears seldom in the lyrics.) See Dunbar, p. 279; but also see Robert W. Frank, "The Art of Reading Medieval Personification Allegory," *ELH*, XX (1953), 243–245.

22. The poem emphasizes the doctrine of the Real Presence more than being a more or less systematized allegorizing of the Mass. If we consider Greene's B version, the hound in stanza six may be the priest at Mass, but the image makes more sense to me as the faithful who drink Christ's blood in the Eucharist.

23. "Forty Hours Devotion," *The Catholic Encyclopedia*, VI, 151. For earlier analogues to this devotion, see Charles V. Finnegan, *Priest's Manual for the Forty Hours Devotion* (Paterson, N.J., 1958), p. 3.

24. Miss Gilchrist and several others discuss the carol in *Journal of the Folk-Song Society*, IV (1910–13), 52–66, esp. pp. 55–59. Greene sums up the chief arguments, pp. 411–412. He has recently advanced a historical interpretation of his own, "The Meaning of the Corpus Christi Carol," *Medium Aevum*, XXIX (1960), 10–21, in which he argues not very convincingly that the weeping and praying "may" in the poem "startlingly" parallels the account of Catharine of Aragon's exile as told by Nicholas Harpsfield. The wounded knight is Christ in the Host, the object of Catharine's devotion from the chapel window; Catharine purportedly wept night and day, and this fact would tend to make almost any contemporary hearer identify her in the "may"; the stone refers to Catharine's weeping on the stones at Buckden.

25. *Medieval English Poetry* (London, 1958), p. 77.

26. See the Sarum Breviary, ed. Francis Procter and Christopher Wordsworth (Canterbury, 1883), I, cccxxx; the York Missal, ed. T. Henderson, Surtees Society, LX (Durham, 1874), pp. 317–318. For elaborate and particularly relevant passages, see Ivo Carnotensis, "De Epiphania Domini," *PL*, CLXII, 574–575; pseudo-Bonaventure, *The Mirrour of the Blessed Lyf* . . . , pp. 54–55. Herebert and his sources may be using an allegorical as well as a tropological sense; some of the analogues cited stress the marriage of Christ with His Church, but what applies to the Church as a whole applies to the individual members, and this twofold interpretation is easily justified.

27. Printed in Thomas Wright and J. O. Halliwell, eds., *Reliquiae Antiquae* (London, 1843), II, 121.

28. Brown reads *aswynde,* "languish away."

29. *The Middle English Dictionary* glosses *cleo* as "? a reaping hook." The word has proved something of a crux, but I am unaware of any more satisfactory interpretation. *Cliff* makes little sense, for it weakens the simile; the sense of rapidity which the other reading gives emphasizes the idea of transitoriness.

30. Rev. xxi. 19–20; the images of the flower and spice have parallels in the Song of Songs.

31. Brown emends to *For on,* although he claims the MS "clearly" reads *ou* (XIII, p. 24). He is supported in his emendation by the reading of the Egerton MS. The second person pronoun makes better sense than the indefinite *one* because it avoids an ambiguity of reference when the poem shifts to *þe* in line 5. *Ou* is, of course, the plural form, but the singular and plural forms often shifted places about this time; see, e.g., Fernand Mossé, *A Handbook of Middle English*, trans. James A. Walker (Baltimore, 1952), p. 94. Cf. the shift from *þe* to *eu* in Thomas of Hales' love ron, line 118.

For may be translated "before," "in the presence of." *Is* is the northern form for *arn* or *are;* to support a northern influence, cf. in the Egerton MS the form *til hym* (line 17) and the rime *sone : bone* (lines 37, 39).

32. References are legion; among the lengthier discussions, see St. Peter Damian, "De Epiphania Domini" I, *PL*, CXLIV, 508; St. Bernard, "Super *Missus Est*" II, *PL*, CLXXXIII, 70; Peter Cellensis, "In Annuntiatione Dominica" III, *PL*, CCII, 714; *Old English Homilies of the Twelfth Century*, ed. Richard Morris, EETS, LIII (London, 1873), p. 161.

33. This concept is popular in Latin hymns; e.g., *AH*, XX, Nos. 27, 43, 137, 191.

34. St. Thomas Aquinas, "In Nativitate BMV," *Opera Omnia*, ed. Petrus Fiaccadoris (New York, 1948–49), XXIV, 232.

35. *AH*, XX, No. 158. In another Latin hymn Mary is called "origo / Virtutis" (*AH*, XLV[a], No. 8); in still another, "Mater virtutis et nostrae causa salutis" (*AH*, L, No. 292).

36. See, e.g., J. M. Campbell, "Patristic Studies and the Literature of Mediaeval England," *Speculum*, VIII (1933), 465–478; D. W. Robertson, "Historical Criticism," English Institute Essays, 1950, ed. Alan S. Downer (New York, 1951), pp. 3–31; Morton W. Bloomfield, "Symbolism in Medieval Literature," *MP*, LVI (1956), 73–81; and the essays by E. Talbot Donaldson, R. E. Kaske, and Charles Donahue in *Critical Approaches to Medieval Literature*, ed. Dorothy Bethurum (New York, 1960), pp. 1–82.

37. Pseudo-Bonaventure, *The Mirrour of the Blessed Lyf . . .* , p. 9.

CHAPTER FIVE

PIETY AND WIT

A modern reader accustomed to the high intellectual voltage of a Donne, a Hopkins, or an Eliot often becomes impatient with the low power of the Middle English religious lyrics. But the modern reader perhaps overlooks the fact that Donne, Hopkins, and Eliot were not deeply influenced by the affective school of piety. Certainly the tendency of such a movement is towards intellectual simplicity and emotional complexity. Yet St. Bernard, one of the founders of the school, was often witty—a quality which not even the uninspired English translator of his "Aspicias capud inclinatum" (XIII, No. 69) can completely submerge. Furthermore, Donne, Hopkins, and Eliot work within the tradition of the dramatic lyric, rather than that of the song; on this basis alone we must expect differences. From one point of view, the song does not invite a deep intellectual content, for the use of wit hinders the characteristic hypnotic effect which the song by definition strives for. Northrop Frye makes this point when he speaks of the "perilous balance in paranomasia between verbal wit and hypnotic incantation. . . . Wit detaches the reader; the oracle absorbs him." [1] Yet the mere fact that a poem soars to glorious heights of sound

does not mean that it must hobble intellectually. For-
tunatus, Adam of St. Victor, and Thomas Aquinas wrote
hymns which soar as gloriously as any song, yet flash with
paradox, antithesis, word-play, and startling comparisons.
The song is perfectly capable of sticking out its tongue
at theorists who rhapsodize about its attention to sound;
it can also dazzle its readers by the way it illumines its
subject matter. Some critics have raised an eyebrow at
finding a trace of something which looks remarkably like
metaphysical wit in the English religious lyrics. They
should be more surprised that the English lyric inherited
so little of the embarrassment of intellectual riches in the
Latin hymn and sermon.

Unfortunately, not only the quantity but also the
quality of this intellectual wealth is sometimes embar-
rassing. Perhaps the English poets felt they were really
beautifying their lyrics, but they sinned grievously against
good taste. One offender reacts thus to Mary's grief for
her dead Son: "Yif wepyng myght rype bee, it semyd
þan in season" (XV, No. 9). Yet critics will praise this
line. Equally effective is Lydgate's anemic "Lyff, sleyng
deth, deyde vpon þe Crose," [2] which offers little to advance the thought of its stanza. In fact Lydgate so lards
the first two stanzas of this poem with incidental paradoxes that he completely loses the flavor of his Latin
original. He is often singularly able to employ wit, as
he does here, to appeal to his audience's grasp of the
mystery involved without either deepening their understanding of it or enhancing their emotional response to it.
In another poem, he has the crucified Jesus advise man:
"Thinke ageyn, pride, on myn humylyte; / Kom to scole,
recorde weell this lessoun." The image resumes a few
lines later: "Afforn thyn herte hang this lytel table,"
and thus underscores the pedantic tone of the poem as
a whole. Education again does not provide a particularly
effective image when it forces "In place as man may se," [3]
an abecedarian poem, into a clever but strained unity.

The speaker carefully points out that when a child goes to school, a book is brought him called an ABC, nailed on a slab of wood and rubricated with five paraffes. The poet then thumps across the significance of the image: by this book we may divine that Christ was nailed on a tree and pierced with five bloody wounds. He then reads the letters one by one, beginning with A. But the ingenuity with which the poet works in all the letters of the alphabet hinders a strong emotive content, and it offers little insight into the Passion and Crucifixion.* This same basically shallow wit sometimes becomes more functional, as in the following brief poem which expresses belief in the Real Presence:

Hyt semes quite and is red;	*white*	
Hyt is quike and semes dede;	*alive*	
Hyt is fleshe and semes bred;		
4 Hyt is on and semes too;	*one*	*two*
Hyt is God body and no more.[4]		

This poem invites comparison with the Anglo-Saxon riddle, but suffers as a result of comparing it with the best of the older poems, for it offers little more than the accepted formulation of its religious truth. It represents a type of poem which, for the most part, draws wearily upon paradox and seems intended for a popular rather than a learned audience. (Brown groups a series of these poems under the general heading of "The Mysteries of the Faith," XV, Nos. 117–121.) Other examples of this type of wit may be seen in the poems of the Franciscan school; they are generally shallow treatments of profound

* Taste, of course, differs over a period of five centuries; these images may have been very effective in their own time. One of James Ryman's lines clearly illustrates this point (Greene, No. 318); referring to Christ as the eucharistic bread, he writes: "In virgyne Mary this brede was bake." A twentieth-century reader will shudder, even if Erich Neumann speaks of "the old proverb, 'The oven is the mother,'" *The Great Mother*, Bollingen Series, XLVII (New York, 1955), p. 286.

ideas and serve not to offer insight, but to arouse emotional response. Time after time we meet the omnipotent God, Creator of heaven and earth, shivering and lying in poverty in a stable, weeping for man's sins—as in the following example (XIV, No. 65):

> Lullay, lullay, litel child; child,
>   reste þe a þrowe,   *while*
> Fro heyȝe hider art þu sent with *from on high*
>   us to wone lowe;   *to dwell*
> Pore & litel art þu mad, vnkut *unrecognized*
>   & vnknowe,
> 4   Pine an wo to suffren her for
>   þing þat was þin owe.
> Lullay, l[ullay] litel child,
>   sorwe mauth þu make;   *must*
> Þu art sent in-to þis werd, as   *world*
>   tu were for-sake.

This lyric illustrates well Walter J. Ong's description of Franciscan poetry:

> No need for striking juxtapositions, for the stimulus of insights freshly arrived at, establishing intricate connections between realities apprehended in all sorts of ways and at all sorts of levels simultaneously —no need for wit in any form. Here the business is that of calling up familiar blocks of feeling and transferring them to a higher plane. Simply exclamation and conspicuous parallelism will do. . . .[5]

The air of mystery which surrounds such poems is not theological mystery;

> it is derived not so much from the dogmatic content of revelation, from the mind's being in contact with truths which it finds too massive for its grasp, as from the somewhat hypnotic repetitiousness and parallelism commonly available for popular incantation. It

is the "mystery" of the eerie, like that in the witches' charms in *Macbeth*. . . .

On the other hand, some of the medieval poets successfully employed wit to analyze either the speaker's emotions or his insight into the subject which he presents, or both. The final line of "Quanne hic se on rode" (XIII, No. 35B) sharply defines the speaker's emotion; he knows that when he meditates upon the crucified Christ he ought to weep and abandon his sins,

> yif hic of luue kan,   *if I*
> yif hic of luue kan,
> 12   yif hic of luue kan.

Three times he states this condition and puns on the meaning. If he can recognize the depths of the great love which Christ has shown for him by His act of redemption, if he can realize the great love shown by Mary and John in standing under the cross (lines 3–4), then he must know that mere weeping and abandoning sins are feeble acts of love indeed. Another example uses wit to reinforce its moral lesson and bears traces of the "metaphysical shudder," anticipating "To his Coy Mistress": "to ded when wow gase, / A grysely geste bese þan þi breste in armes til enbrase" [when you go to death, a grisly guest is then your breast in arms to embrace] (XIV, No. 81, lines 33–34). A third example underscores both the speaker's emotion and the religious subject matter; the following lines borrow from exegetical tradition and pun on sleep as sleep, spiritual lethargy, sin, and death (XIII, No. 2): [6]

> Slep me haꝺ mi lif forstole,
>   richt half oꝺer more;
> awai! to late ich was iwar, nu   *aware*
>   hit me reoweꝺ sore.   *I rue*
> in slepe ne wende ich endie   *I did not expect*

nocht þech ich slepe   *to end   though*
euremore;
hwao-se lifeð þat wakerur *whoever more watchful*
12   beo, þencþ of mine lore.   *think   instruction*

Al to longe slepð þe mann þat
neure nele awakie;   *will not awaken*
hwo-se understant wel his ende-
dai, wel ȝeorne he mot   *very eagerly*
spakie   *hasten*
to donde sunne awei fram him   *put sin*
& fele almesse makie,   *many almsdeeds*
16   ȝif him ne schal, hwanne he   *when*
forð-want, his brei-gurdel *goes forth (dies)*
quakie.

There is a gentle irony here; now that the speaker has
aged, he offers others the good advice which he himself
would not previously accept. He realizes now the importance of a good life and warns man that he had better
confess his sins and give alms if he doesn't expect, when
he dies, to quake in his breeches! Through his use of wit,
the author enhances the audience's conception of sin. If
such wit does not dazzle, it at least glows.

More luminous wit, which penetrates further the
religious subject matter, may be seen in several isolated
examples. One poet employs a striking use of paradox
in speaking of Mary (Greene, No. 30): "That euer was
thralle, now ys he fre; / That euer was smalle, now grete
is she." By emphasizing the parallelism between the two
lines, the poet reminds us of Mary's role in freeing man
from the bonds of sin. By punning on the physiological
and spiritual meanings of the second line, the poet focuses his paradox on Mary's humility and her consequent elevation to Mother of God. (According to medieval authors, God made Mary His mother primarily
because of her humility, and only secondarily because of

her chastity.) By reversing in the second half of the line the word order of the first half, the poet heightens the transformation of which he speaks. Also treating Mary's singularity is a series of witty lines in "Edi beo þu, heuene quene" (XIII, No. 60, lines 49–56). The paradox in the first four lines is twofold, but the author follows familiar paths in presenting it: Mary, a maid without sexual mate, bore within the tiny space of her womb Him Whom the whole world might not encompass. The following lines allude to the widespread notion that Mary, unlike Eve, conceived without sin (thus continuing the notion of virginity in lines 49–50) and consequently gave birth without pain: "Þe ne stiȝte [pierced] ne þe ne priȝte [pricked] / in side, in lende [loins], ne elleswhere [elsewhere]." The poet then elaborates this notion by punning on the name of Jesus. It is only fitting that Mary gave birth without pain, for she bore Jesus, Whose name means "healer." [7] Sometimes it is the Crucifixion scene which the poet's wit illumines; in the following example (XIII, No. 47), the speaker addresses Mary at the foot of the cross, and puns on the actual event (Matt. xxvii.45) and its symbolic significance:

þe brithe day went in-to nith	*turned into night*
þo ihesu crist, þin herte lith,	*when light*
was iqueint with pine and wo.	*extinguished*

The poet not only deepens his audience's conception of Mary's grief; he also suggests the theological implications of the act of crucifixion by the ever-widening connotations of Christ as light.

When the medieval poet uses wit, he may merely ornament an inherently valuable subject much as he may employ an elaborate sound structure; or he may heighten his audience's emotional response to the truth; or he may actually deepen his audience's understanding of the religious mystery. The poetry of wit in Middle English com-

prises a larger corpus than most commentators have
realized. Examples of wit are not only incidental, as we
have just observed, but characteristic of entire poems.
Sometimes the poem is short, as the following:

> Blodles & bonles, blod has nou
> bon;
> Fadur had fadur þᵗ ffadur has
> non;
> þe werk & werkmon, hoe ben   *they are*
> al on;   *one*
> 4   He þᵗ neuer ne ede, ffyrryste   *went first*
> had y-gon.[8]

This poem has been misread as "lines on the Host"; the
subject is instead the Incarnation of the Second Person
of the Trinity. Bloodless and boneless because incor-
poreal, blood (in the sense of "kindred," i.e., the Son) now
has assumed flesh. Since the Trinity is indivisible, the
entire Trinity is present in Christ's divine nature; therefore, God the Father, Who has no father, had St. Joseph
as father (notice the use of tenses). Line 3 refers, of course,
to God as creator and as creation (man). Line 4 expresses
God's omnipresence. Since God is present everywhere,
the Second Person, Who left heaven to become man,
never really left. The quatrain thus examines cleverly,
but perceptively, the paradox of the God-Man.

As we may readily suspect, the English poets who
used wit often exploited the rich tradition of imagery
at their disposal. One poet uses as a basic image that of
Christ's body as a present to man. The idea may have
been suggested by John iii.16; certainly the poet repeats
the familiar Johannine concept of God as Love. The
poem perhaps verges on the borderline of true wit and
does not always succeed, but its use of puns and paradoxes make it an interesting example of the Middle English poetry of wit (XIV, No. 90):

Crist makiþ to man a fair
 present,

His blody body wiþ loue brent;   *burnt*

Þat blisful body his lyf haþ
 lent,

4 For loue of man þat synne haþ
 blent.   *blinded*

 O Loue, loue, what hast þou
  ment?

 Me þinkeþ þat loue to wraþþe
  is went.   *turned*

Þi loueliche hondis loue haþ   *lovely*
 to-rent,

8 And þi liþe arme[s] wel streit
 itent;   *stretched*

Þi brest is baar, þi bodi is bent,

for wrong haþ wonne & riȝt is
 schent.   *put to shame*

Þi mylde boones loue haþ
 to-drawe,

12 Þe naylis þi feet han al
 to-gnawe;   *gnawed to pieces*

Þe lord of loue loue haþ now
 slawe—   *slain*

Whane loue is strong it haþ no
 lawe.

His herte is rent, / his body is
 bent

16 vpon þe roode tre;

Wrong is went, / þe deuel is   *turned aside*
 schent,   *discomfited*

 crist, þurȝ þe myȝt of þee.

For þee þat herte is leyd to
 wedde;   *as pledge*

20   swych was þe loue þat herte vs
            kedde,   *made known*

        Þat herte barst, þat herte
            bledde,

        Þat herte blood oure soulis
            fedde.

        Þat herte clefte for treuþe of
            loue,

24   Þerfore in him oon is trewe   *alone*
            loue;

        For loue of þee þat herte is
            ȝoue;   *given*

        Kepe þou þat herte & þou art
            aboue.

        Loue, loue, where schalt þou
            wone?   *dwell*

28   Þi wonyng-stede is þee bi-nome,   *taken from you*

        For cristis herte þat was þin
            hoome—

        He is deed, now hast þou
            noone.

            Loue, loue, whi doist þou so?

32   Loue, þou brekist myn herte
            a-two.

        Loue haþ schewid his greet
            myȝt,

        For loue haþ maad of day þe
            nyȝt;

        Loue haþ slawe þe kyng of ryȝt,

36   And loue haþ endid þe strong
            fiȝt.

        So Inliche loue was neuere   *heartfelt*
            noon;

Þat witiþ wel marie & Ioon,
And also witen þei euerychon,
40   Þat loue wiþ hym is maad at
         oon.

Loue makiþ, crist, þin herte
         myn,
So makiþ loue myn herte þin;
Þanne schulde myn be trewe al
         tym,
44   And loue in loue schal make it
         fyn.

Although the poem is loosely constructed, the poet gives
it an imagistic unity, punning on three meanings of
Christ's body as a present to man. In the first section of
the poem (lines 1–18) the image refers to Christ's actual
body as man, and this section therefore contemplates the
Crucifixion. The second section (lines 19–26), with its
emphasis upon the heart and blood of Christ, suggests
a second way in which Christ's body is present—through
the Holy Eucharist. The third section (lines 27–44),
emphasizing both the heart and the dwelling place, suggests a third way—mystical union. These three aspects
of the image of the present, however, remain in outline;
the poet does not stress them, as he might easily have
done. The epithet *brent* (line 2) describes the love Christ
has for man and thus serves as the basis for the personification of Love as the slayer of Christ. It also suggests a
holocaust, and thus prepares for the suggestion of the
Eucharist in the second section, emphasizing the fact
that this sacrifice of the New Law replaces the burnt
offerings of the Old. The word *wedde* (line 19) implies
that Christ's sacrifice on the cross was a pledge of His
promise to give us His flesh to eat and His blood to drink.
The image of the present as Christ's body on the cross
thus coalesces with the image as the Eucharist. The third

section prepares for the third meaning of the present by using the image of the dwelling place. Love has no place to stay, says the speaker, since Christ is dead; but then he finds a dwelling place for love in Mary and John and everyone who is made one with Christ (lines 37–40). The speaker then asks that his heart be made a dwelling place for love (line 42), but with an intensity that the image of the dwelling place suggests but weakly. Since this emotion is more intense, the poet suggests both the image of possession and of a refining process, with its attendant connotations of intense heat and purification. The word *trewe* (line 43) thus has multiple connotations; it recalls the concept of true love (line 24) and relates to *fyn* (line 44), which in turn recalls something of the ennobling troubadour concept of *fin amour*. Since the thought of this last stanza is expressed in such forceful terms, the relationship between Christ and the soul refers to more than an ordinary exchange of love, and suggests mystical union. Union with God is, of course, the whole purpose behind the gift of His body to man, and this last stanza very strikingly concludes the sequence in the triple meaning of the image.

The first and third sections pun heavily on *love* as the personified abstraction, as the love Christ felt for man, as the emotion felt by Mary, St. John, and the speaker—then all these meanings absorb into Christ Himself as Love, the source of all love. The paradoxes of the first section are climaxed when the speaker sees in love its opposite—wrath—and recognizes that love has become so extreme that it has slain the Lord of Love (lines 13–14). Therefore "wrong haþ wonne & riȝt is schent" (line 10), but at the same time the lawlessness of love only proves its nature, and the poet completes the paradox—it took a great wrong to right a great wrong (lines 17–18). The parallelism of lines 17 and 10 underscore their paradoxical relationship. Another aspect of excessive love appears in the third section (lines 33–36) and continues the paradoxical relationships set up in the first. Love is so powerful that it turned day into night, slew the King of Right, and ended the warfare between man and the devil. But this excessive love is personified in Christ Himself, so that the speaker in effect tells us that Love slew Himself through His own volition. This ties in with the suggestion in section two of the image of the pelican which tears open her breast and feeds her young with her own blood—a type of Christ (lines 21-22).[9] This elaborate punning reflects the multiple meanings of the image of the present and reinforces their interrelationship. Just as the tropological meaning (mystical union) reflects the allegorical (the Eucharist) and both center in the ultimate historical reality of the Crucifixion, so the ever-widening puns on *love* center in Christ, the ultimate Reality.

We have already noticed in passing the opulent wit in the medieval Latin hymns. On the basis of surviving texts we can observe that only a very few of the wittiest were translated into English; the few that were translated, the translators garbled. One exception, however, is a successful translation of the fairly witty Latin sequence, "Stabat iuxta Christi crucem" (see appendix). The English version captures the wit of the original, but makes several interesting changes. The text (XIII, No. 4) is as follows:

		stod ho þere neh			*stood she there nearby*
	Þat	leueli leor wid spald ischent,			*lovely face with spittle marred*
	þat	feire fel wid s[cur]ges rend—			*skin*
		Þe blod out stremed oueral.			
4		Skoarn, upbraid, and schome speche:			*shameful*

al hit was to sorhes eche—   *increase*
    i woa þu was biluken al.   *woe you (Mary)*
                                              encompassed

I þat blisful bearnes buirde   *birth*
8   wrong w[e]s wroht to wom-
                mone wirde,   *destiny*
        ah kuinde craued nou þe   *but nature*
            riht.
    Þenne þu loch, ah nou þu   *laughed*   *but now*
        wep;
    þi wa wes waken, þat tenne   *then*
        slep—
12   childing-pine haues te nou *childbirth pains*
            picht.   *pierced*

Nou þu moostes, lauedi, lere   *learn*
    wmmone wo þat barnes   *of women*   *children*
        bere,
        þa bit[t]er and ta bale þrehes;   *baleful throes*
16 For in his dead þe wo þu ȝulde   *death*   *yielded*
    in childing þat tu þole schulde   *suffer*
        þurd modres kuindeliche   *natural*
            lahes.   *laws*

Ah, lauedi, þah þu wonges wete,   *cheeks wet*
20 þah þe were wo at unimete,   *in excess*
        þine loates weren lasteles; *deceits* *blameless*
    Þi wep ne wemmede noht þin   *grief*   *impair*
            heau   *appearance*
    þat made þi leor ful louk and   *face*   *feeble*
            lew—   *wan*
24   swa sari wmmon neuer neas.   *=ne was*

Ah þi kare was ouer-comen;   *but*
    þe þridde dai þi ioie comen,
        ded and deuel driuen doun   *death*

28   Þwen þi son risen wes
      to þine wele and ure peas—   *welfare*
      blisse he brocte in icha toun.   *brought   each*

      Þi luue sone uprisinge   *resurrection*
32   was selli liik to his birdinge—   *birth*
      bi-twene twa his litel   *two is*
            schead—   *distinction*
      For, so gleam glidis þurt þe
            glas,
      of þi bodi born he was,
36   and þurt þe hoale þurch he   *whole tomb*
            gload.   *glided*

      Milde moder, maiden oa,   *always*
      of al þi kare come þou þoa   *then*
      hwen þi sone rise wes.   *risen*
40   Leuedi, bring us out of wa,
      of sinne, of sorhe, of sich   *sighing*
            al-swoa,   *also*
            to bliss þat his endeles.
            AM[EN].

Although the MS evidence seems to favor reading the
first four words as the conclusion of a preceding stanza,[10]
it is tempting to consider the poem as complete and the
four words as translating the Latin title. The first four
Latin stanzas contribute only indirectly to the paradoxical theme of this poem—the contrast between Mary's
joy and pain at the birth and death of her Son. The purpose of the omitted four stanzas is the same as that of
the fifth in the original (stanza one of our poem), summed
up in line 6: "i woa þu was biluken al." In our poet's
second stanza we meet the paradox that Mary bore Christ
without pain, but now nature takes vengeance and mul-
tiplies Mary's grief at her Son's death. The paradox thus
accents the relationship between life and death; it sug-

gests the notion of rebirth, which the sixth stanza explicitly develops. The poet speaks of Mary's preservation
from pain as a wrong wrought to woman's destiny, and
nature now craves that this wrong be righted (lines 8–9).
The next stanza develops this thought. In the fourth
stanza, the speaker feels that Mary's deceits against nature were blameless; she did not, in other words, deliberately set out to cheat nature (this notion is not
found in the original). But besides bringing forth her
Son without pain, Mary conceived without sin or shame,
so that she has also tricked nature by her virgin maternity. Lines 22–23 develop the parallel between this aspect
of her childbearing and her beholding her dead Son: her
weeping, as her conceiving, has not stained Mary's chaste
physical appearance but has instead simply made her
face pale and wan. (The Latin stanza 8b is more suggestive in the verb *deflorat.*) Her joy in the birth of Christ
is now paralleled by His resurrection (stanza five)—that
is, His rebirth (stanza six)—and in the concluding stanza
the speaker wishes that we, as Mary, may pass from sorrow (this life) to joy (heaven). Indeed, the poet implies
the parallel of our own rebirth through Mary our Mother
into everlasting joy.

The English poet has made three important altera-
tions in his original. The first is the omission of the image
in the sixth stanza of the Latin (stanza two in our poem);
another translator (XIII, No. 47) has kept the image:

Nu he hoschet with		*it*	(*nature*) *asks*
goulinge			*usurious interest*
þat þu im in þi chil-	*what*	*from it*	*child-*
tinge			*bearing*
36 al withelde þar biforn.			

Our poet has chosen to omit this image and instead emphasize the contrast between Mary's childbirth and her
agony at her Son's death. He has therefore introduced an
extremely witty line: "Þenne þu loch, ah nou þu wep"

(line 10). This laughter not only reinforces the concept of her joy at Christ's birth and makes it contrast more strongly with her present agony, but also refers to her miraculous conceiving of Christ. In the Old Testament, Sarah, the wife of Abraham, was at an advanced age when she conceived her son; this mark of divine favor was considered a prototype of Mary's miraculous conceiving. When Sarah was told that she would conceive, she laughed because she was so old (Gen. xviii.12). Her son was named Isaac, a pun on *he laughs;* medieval poets consequently referred to Christ as Sarah's laughter.[11] Since the word *loch* is a stronger word than the context demands, it should be read with the implications I have indicated: Mary was singularly favored by God and was exempted by a special grace from the course of certain natural events. Read with these connotations, the image ingeniously fits the total context of the poem. The final important change which our poet has made is the strengthening of the Nativity-Resurrection parallels, thus reinforcing the notions of birth and rebirth. Just as Mary rejoiced at the birth of Christ, so now she rejoices at His rebirth. Our poet has used the ubiquitous sun-glass image, but the context here gives it a new vitality. This image looks back to the suggestion of the virgin maternity in lines 22–24; it also connects the notion of the subtlety (spirituality, penetrability) of Christ's risen body with the mystery of the Incarnation. Our poet has used the same verb in both instances, *glidis* (line 34) and *gload* (line 36), to underscore this relationship, and the two mysteries mutually illumine each other.[12] The request in the last stanza has been prepared for by stanza five; the reference to the descent into hell further reinforces the concept of rebirth. By his changes, then, our poet shows himself as perceptively witty as the Latin author.

This use of wit to illumine the religious subject matter may sometimes be found in the carol—for example,

the following (Greene, No. 173), one of the most justly
admired carols of the period:

> [T]her [is n]o rose of swych
>   vertu
> As is the rose that bare Jhesu.
>
> Ther is no ro[se of] swych vertu
> As is the rose that bar Jhesu;
>   Alleluya.
>
> 4   For in this rose conteynyd was
>   Heuen and erthe in lytyl space:
>   Res miranda.
>
> Be that rose we may weel see
> 8   That he is God in personys
>   thre,
>   Pari forma.
>
> The aungelys sungyn, the shep-
>   erdes to: *too*
> "Gloria in excelcis Deo."
> 12   Gaudeamus.
>
> [L]eue we al this wordly
>   merthe,
> And folwe we this joyful
>   berthe;
>   Transeamus!

Although the rose is one of the most popular images
used for the Virgin Mary, our poet subordinates all the
multiple connotations of the symbol to an explicit basis
but still puns: "Ther is no rose of swych vertu." *Vertu*
is ambiguous; one meaning may be "excellence." Applied
to the Virgin it refers to the theological sense of *virtue,*
for throughout the Middle Ages the Virgin is praised as

possessing every virtue to a superlative degree. Another meaning may be *power,* specifically, power of generation, as in a Latin hymn (*AH,* IX, No. 89):

> Tu es rosa, cujus nodo
> Latens fluxit miro modo
> Palliata deitas.

These meanings, however, are subordinate to a third—a medicinal sense. The medicinal values of the rose were so well known that a poet of the late fourteenth century comments:

Of þe rose þat spryngyth on spray
[And] schewyth hys flowris in someres
    day—
It nedyth noȝt him to discrie,   *describe*
Eueri man knowyth at ye   *eye*
Of his vertues and of his kinde.[13]   *powers*   *nature*

The author of a fourteenth-century French *plantaire* thus naturally enough sees in the rose and its medicinal qualities a symbol of Mary. Of the virtue of the rose he sums up: "Rose est de ml't grant efficace / Plurieurs maladies respasse." [14] In his application of this image to Mary he concludes: "Marie en toute affliction / Nous est *in adiutorium*" (Lines 108–109). Our poet, however, in applying the sanative powers of the rose to Mary, thinks of her as the bearer of Jesus, as in a contemporary lyric: "To owr helth thou bar a chyld" (Greene, No. 206, line 5). Behind the thought of lines 1–2 lies the ambiguity of the Latin *salus,* which means both health and salvation. Mary, in bringing us salvation, brought us health as well; her sanative powers thereby exceed those of any natural rose, and therefore we should rejoice. Thus the first stanza concludes on a liturgical note of joy: "Alleluia."

    The second stanza explains by a paradox why there is no rose of such virtue. To the familiar contrast in the Middle Ages between the God Who created heaven and

earth and all things, and the God-Man Who lay in the
womb of the Virgin, our poet gives new emphasis; he
tells us that within this rose were contained both heaven
and earth (lines 4–5).[15] In other words, within the small
space of Mary's womb, heaven joins earth and God becomes man. Within our poet's deceptively simple stanza
he is able, by means of this paradox, to convey something
of the mystery inherent in the Incarnation, and he
comments: "Res miranda" (line 6). The tension between
the simplicity of statement and the deep religious mystery of the subject matter continues in the next stanza.
Here we have the central mystery of Christianity brought
before our eyes: through the efficacy of that rose we may
see the Trinity, not figuratively, but in actuality. *We*
may be used here in a generic sense to indicate mankind;
in this Child Whom Mary bore we also may see the Trinity, but not as the shepherds. We may see the Child as
they did only if we use our imaginations; but as a fifteenth-century poet mentions, Christ is visible to us
every day at Mass under the form of bread and wine
(XV, No. 115). But however we see this Child, we see
Him because He appeared in the same shape (*Pari
forma*) as "that rose," i.e., in human flesh. And in seeing
Him, we see the entire Trinity as well, for the Trinity
is indivisible; "Blessed be the Holy Trinity, and undi-
vided unity" states the Introit of the Mass of the Holy
Trinity. The major emphasis in the poem thus far is
upon the mystery of God become man, but the poet reminds us that this was accomplished through Mary ("*By*
that rose"). His use of the word *that* relegates Mary's
role to the background as the mystery and our seeing it
take the foreground. This contrasts with line 4, where
the word *this* brings greater stress to Mary's role.

Up to this point there have been two major motifs
in the poem: the salvation of man, the cause of our joy;
and the fusion of heaven and earth in God become man.
In stanza four these two concepts blend, that of heaven

and earth in the angels and the shepherds; and that of joy in the songs of the angels and shepherds, and in the final injunction, "Gaudeamus" (line 12). In the fifth stanza these concepts are developed further. Here "we" are invited to become present-day shepherds; "Transeamus," urges the poet (line 15), which is the word the shepherds said to one another (Luke ii.15). As lines 7–8 tell us, Christ was born for us to see, as well as the shepherds: "Behold I bring you tidings of great joy, which shall be to *all* the people . . ." (Luke ii.10). This message is echoed in our poet's phrase "joyful berthe" (line 14). Stanzas two and three have spoken of God's coming to us; in stanza five we are exhorted to go to God. As Aelfric remarked in a sermon: "We should imitate these shepherds and give praise and honor to our Lord in all things which He performed for our love." [16] Perhaps *transeamus* includes something of the ambiguity which St. Bonaventure ascribes to it. In a spiritual sense, he says, there is a fourfold transition, viz., from ignorance to wisdom, from sin to penitence, from penitence to abundant justice, from misery to glory.[17] Thus *transeamus* exhorts us to complete the cycle begun at Christ's birth; God descended that we might ascend. In the words of the priest at Mass: we become "partakers of His divinity who vouchsafed to become partaker of our humanity." We are called not to worldly, therefore transitory, joy, but to true, spiritual, perfect joy.[18] The poet exhorts his audience to rejoice and to complete the cycle—to partake of the divine nature as God partook of theirs. He deepens their realization that the entire cycle has been made possible through Mary. It is she who has brought this salvation, this spiritual health, and because she has, "Ther is no rose of swych vertu / As is the rose that bar Jhesu."

A final example of the poetry of wit is its finest achievement in the Middle English period (XV, No. 81): [19]

I Syng of a myden
   þat is makeles;
kyng of alle kynges
4   to her son che ches.   *as her son she chose*

he cam also stylle
   þer his moder was   *where*
as dew in aprylle
8   þat fallyt on þe gras.

he cam also stylle
   to his moderes bowr
as dew in aprille
12   þat fallyt on þe flour.

he cam also stylle
   þer his moder lay
as dew in aprille
16   þat fallyt on þe spray.

moder & mayden
   was neuer non but che—
wel may swych a lady
20   godes moder be.

Perhaps the first thing we note about this poem is the
tone of wonder and exultation in Mary's dual role as
maiden and mother. A similar tone was often used in
speaking of the virgin-motherhood of Mary, and although
a sense of the miracle involved is often part of this tone,
there is rarely any attempt at explanation.[20] The general
attitude is that of the Middle English preacher toward
the man of authority, knowledge, and holiness:

> be not to be to inquisitiff how þat itt may be þat
> þe virginite and þe moderhede be bothe in oure
> Lady, for þe cause her-of beþ not of common nature

but of Goddes wurchynge and is hiʒe myracle and
abowen þe common cours of kynde.[21]

Our poet, on the other hand, while achieving a tone of
exultation partly by the incremental repetition in stanzas
2–4, is at the same time explaining how it was possible
for Mary to bear a child yet remain a virgin. He explains
in terms of what the preacher just quoted called "Goddes
wurchynge" and "hiʒe myracle"; he explains through his
imagery the theological and natural implications of this
great mystery. Much of the tone of wonder and exultation arises, in fact, from our poet's realization of the
factors involved in this mystery of Mary's virgin-maternity—an event which might cause even our own jaundiced
age to pause momentarily in wonder.

The poem divides into three parts. The first part
(stanza one) announces the theme: "I syng of a myden
/ þat is makeles." The second part (stanzas two to four)
proves the theme, but not by the "naive tautology" of
which Leo Spitzer speaks.[22] The third part (stanza five)
sums up the proof by the restatement of theme: "moder
and mayden / was neuer non but che," then extends this
restatement by summing up imagistic motifs found earlier
in the poem.

The announcement of theme contains an important
ambiguity. *Makeles* means "matchless," as editors usually
gloss it, but this is a secondary meaning derived from its
primary meaning of "without mate," i.e., sexual mate.[23]
The singularity of this maiden is emphasized by the rime-
stress on the privative suffix. Our poet, then, announces
he is singing of a maiden who is without a mate and thus
calls immediate attention to her virginity. When we
read the last line of stanza one we find that this virgin
has chosen a son, and we are startled. Our poet has
heightened his paradox by a shift in tense from line 2
to line 4: the maiden *is* without a mate, yet she *chose*

a son. And it is precisely because this maiden had a son
without benefit of sexual mate that she is matchless.
This is an excellent illustration of Father Ong's comments on the use of the pun in the medieval poetry of
wit; puns are used, he says,

> for serious effects—that is, puns are used to another
> purpose than that of giving a *prima facie* startling
> appearance to essentially drab fact. Puns are used
> where semantic coincidence penetrates to startling
> relations in the real order of things (p. 315).

Apart from developing Mary's matchlessness as derived
from her matelessness, line 4 reinforces her supremacy
by paraphrasing her *fiat* as "che ches." Underscoring
this matchlessness still further is the reference to Christ
in line 3 as the King of Kings, and the maiden would
have to be matchless indeed to choose Him as her Son.

In the first stanza, then, our poet has announced that
he sings of a maiden who is mateless and thereby matchless. Stanzas two to four develop the theme of her matelessness and at the same time prove her matchlessness.
If Mary conceived without sexual intercourse, the question is how she did conceive, and our poet answers in
three parts.

> He cam also stylle
> þer his moder was
> as dew in aprylle
> þat fallyt on þe gras

is the first part of his answer. Dew is, of course, a conventional symbol of the Holy Spirit and His grace. This,
then, is how Mary conceived—through the grace of the
Holy Spirit, recalling Luke i.35. The poet uses the symbol of the dew three times, however. Every well-informed
Christian knew that although a particular act was attributed to the Holy Spirit, that act was the work of the

entire Trinity, for the Trinity is indivisible. Here, for example, are the comments of the author of the *Myroure of Our Lady:*

> For thoughe oure lord iesu cryste onely were made man. yet the incarnacion of hym was wroughte by all thre persones. for the outwarde dedes and warkes of the blyssed Trinitye ar vndepartable. and all that one dothe. all thre dothe. for they thre are one.[24]

The threefold occurrence of the dew image in our poem, then, has a doctrinal significance; Mary could conceive a child and remain a virgin through the operation of the Trinity. She was therefore mateless and thereby matchless.

The dew image, however, has multiple connotations which further support the poet's theme. One medieval author sums up the properties of dew frequently mentioned: "Dew cools, makes fecund, moistens, penetrates, cleanses, enters silently, pre-announces the heat and serenity of the day." [25] All of these properties become connotations of the image in our poem. The fecund property of dew (i.e., God's grace) is seen in the progression from grass to flower to spray. When applied to the Virgin Mary, however, the quality of fecundity is modified by the corresponding quality of virginity; just as dew makes fecund and cleanses, so also the grace of God. The silence with which dew falls has also been identified with Mary's virginity: Christ descended into Mary's womb without the movement of concupiscence.[26] Mary, in her act of conceiving miraculously,* was unlike other women in that there was not the slightest trace of concupiscence—one more aspect of her matchlessness.

---

* The doctrine of the virgin birth has been clearly defined for centuries; this doctrine is sometimes confused with the Immaculate Conception (Mary's preservation at conception from the least stain of sin), which caused much controversy in the thirteenth and fourteenth centuries.

But the dew image may also refer to Christ, since by the wording of the simile, *he* in line 5 may equal *dew* in line 7. This also is conventional; Rupert, for instance, glosses Osee xiv.6 so that Christ becomes the dew and Mary the lily (*PL,* CLXVIII, 201). All of the connotations pertaining to Christ are related to the poet's general theme, for Mary's matchlessness is manifest in her choosing such a Son. Most of the connotations which pertain to Christ are related to His act of redemption, and of course to Mary's role in redemption. The most obvious connection between the dew image and Christ is the descent from Heaven, of God becoming man, and Mary's consequent bearing the God-Man. Christ's coming, moreover, was *still,* as our poet comments in line 5. In one sense the thought here is similar to a scriptural passage often glossed with reference to the Incarnation: "For while all things were in quiet silence, and the night was in the midst of her course, Thy almighty word leapt down from heaven from thy royal throne" (Wis. xviii.14–15).[27] We may see in this image of stillness a reference to Christ's humility in that He came in silence, not with any fanfare as would befit an earthly king. We may see further, with a basis in St. Ambrose, a reference to Christ's coming in silence so that the world would not know of His coming, that the worldly would not confuse His spiritual mission with a temporal one.[28] But the image may connote as well something of the awfulness of the act of Incarnation: the silence is reverent—both fearing and ineffable. Perhaps, too, there is a suggestion of the dual nature of God according to some commentators, a paradox of tranquility and activity—"perfect stillness, perfect fecundity," according to John Ruysbroeck.[29]

A further connotation of dew is that it preannounces the warmth of the day, which is glossed as eternal life.[30] Morning has definite connotations that fuse with the idea of redemption. It is allied to the image of Christ as the

sun, or as light, Who drives away the darkness of sin.
It has also the suggestion of a beginning, just as the
Incarnation began the redemption of mankind. And as
Spitzer comments upon another connotation: "The cool
freshness of the morning dew is allowed to convey to
us the idea of the moral *refrigerium,* or the rejuvenation,
brought to humanity by the Redeemer" (p. 155). Similar
connotations surround the image of April in line 7.
April also has the sense of beginning, of rejuvenation,
in contrast to the winter of "mankind's unredeemed age."
These connotations, plus the fact that the feast of the
Annunciation is celebrated the eighth Kalends of April,
are noted by Adam in his *Mariale*.[31] These images, then,
of April, morning, and dew, with their connotations of
redemption, Mary's role in redemption, and her miraculous conceiving, circle around the poet's theme of Mary's
matchlessness.

We have already noted the sequence from grass to
flower to spray in connection with the fecund property
of dew. Matching this progression is the spatial-temporal
sequence in the second line of each of the middle stanzas;
as Spitzer has pointed out:

> the line "there his mother was" . . . indicates a
> minimum of locality, merely the fact that there was
> a place where Mary was; the line "to his mother's
> bower" provides an environment that befits a noble-
> woman (a "lady"); and finally the line "there his
> mother lay" delicately suggests the bed of child-
> birth (p. 156).

Matching these two progressions is a third, involving the
connotations of the images of the grass, flower, and spray.
Each is a simile for the Virgin, and the connotations of
each reveal why Mary is matchless. The flower image
has several related connotations. It is a term of general
excellence: the flower is the choice part of the plant.
More specifically, it is a symbol of beauty. In speaking

maskelles (spotless) and *makeles*. Neither commentator discusses the structural importance of the pun, however. The pun could conceivably also appear in our poet's thirteenth-century source, but the earlier poet does not utilize it structurally, as does our poet. Professors Kenneth R. Pringle and Paul A. Olson have both suggested to me that our poet may also be punning on the Latin *sine macula*.

24. Ed. John Henry Blunt, EETS ES, XIX (London, 1905), p. 94. Among other references may be cited St. Augustine, *Enchiridion*, I, 38, *PL*, XL, 251; Aelfric, "Annunciatio S. Mariae," *Sermones Catholici*, I, 196.

25. Peter Cellensis, "In Annuntiatione Dominica," VI, *PL*, CCII, 721. Discussions of the dew image appear frequently in commentaries upon, and in sermons which allude to, Judges vi.37–40 and Ps. lxxi.6. The qualities of dew mentioned in these passages are those mentioned also in, e.g., *De Bestiis et Aliis Rebus*, IV, *PL*, CLXXVII, 158; Vincent of Beauvais, I, 205. Another quality of dew is sweetness, which applies particularly to Jesus; several ME poems are on this subject. A particularly lengthy discussion of this image appears in St. Anthony of Padua, "In Annuntiatione B M," *Sermones*, ed. Antonius Maria Locatelli (Padua, 1895–1913), pp. 707–709. See also the discussion by Barbara Raw, "'As Dew in Aprille,'" *MLR*, LV (1960), 411–414.

26. Amadeus, *De Maria Virginea Matri*, III, *PL*, CLXXXVIII, 1316–17.

27. An interesting exegesis of this passage appears in Alcuin's sermon on the three silences, *PL*, XLV, 1177, in which he puns on Jesus as the Word of God breaking the second silence. Many other liturgical passages come to mind when reading this poem (the "Rorate, caeli, desuper" versicle, for example), but I have not attempted to discuss the liturgical sources or analogues.

28. "Hodierna igitur die secundum carnem natus est Dominus, ita secreto, ita silentio, ut ortum ejus saeculum penitus ignoraret. Ignoravit enim saeculum; quia et extra conscientiam patris natus est, et extra ordinem naturae conceptus. . . . Sic igitur natus est Dominus, ut ortum ejus nemo futurum suspicaretur, nemo crederet, nemo sentiret. Quemadmodum crederent hoc futurum, quod posteaquam factum est, factum esse vix credunt?" "De Natali Domini" III, *PL*, XVII, 634.

29. *De Vera Contemplatione*, XII, quoted by Underhill, p. 37, in a discussion of this point.

30. Peter Cellensis, col. 721.

31. "Unde cum aperiatur terra, et germinet Salvatorem, primum mensem anni mundum renovantis ad gratiam, quemdam Aprilem

possumus appellare. Aprilis enim (quia Aprilis dicitur quod ad producenda rerum germina matris terrae gremium tali in tempore aperitur) huic mysterio [the Incarnation] congruit, quod haec solemnitas tempore veris, et octavo Kalend. Aprilis celebratur. Hac enim die, et hoc in tempore, ad pluviam angelicae salutationis se humilitatis virgineae sinus aperuit, et de Spiritu sancto Virgo concipiens, tamquam virga floruit" (PL, CCXI, 709).

32. E.g., St. Bernard, "Super Missus Est," I, PL, CLXXXIII, 58; pseudo-Bernard, De Statu Virginum, PL, CLXXXIV, 798; Hali Meidenhad, ed. F. J. Furnivall, EETS, XVIII (rev. ed.; London, 1922), p. 62; pseudo-Bonaventure, The Mirrour of the Blessed Lyf . . . , pp. 30–31.

33. Liber de Nominibus Hebraicis, PL, XXIII, 886.

34. For discussion of the five letters in Maria, see AH, XXX, No. 58; John Bromyard, Part II, pp. 7–8; Lydgate, "Haile, blissed lady," lines 113–135, Minor Poems, p. 303. Number symbolism may be divided into three kinds: structural (the three central stanzas of our poem), appropriate (our poem's five stanzas), and arbitrary (such as Walafrid Strabo's choice of 84 lines for one of his poems because that was the age of the prophetess Anna at Christ's birth). For the last example, and for further discussion of the latter two kinds, see Curtius, pp. 504–509.

CONCLUSION

As "I Syng of a myden" rather aptly demonstrates, the Middle English religious lyric is not the most irrelevant thing in nature, nor a blot on the scutcheon of English literature. But it has generally suffered the reception tendered a poor relation. With all its faults, it deserves respect—not because it is a curiosity or an antique, but because it has a rightful place in the hierarchy of good English poetry. If it shares the negative qualities of the Elizabethan lyric, with its limited subject matter, restricted imagery, generally light intellectual content, and "peculiar impersonal nature," [1] it compares very favorably in more positive ways. Of course there are differences, and important ones. It is an oversimplification—and an inaccuracy—to say that the Renaissance lyric has more technique than substance, while the medieval lyric has more substance than technique. Yet the comparison does admit some truth. The courtly Renaissance poet had every reason to be more conscious of technique than the medieval monk or minstrel. He had the advantage of new literary and musical forms, a greater training in musical and literary theory, and a subject matter which required more technique than insight. The shepherds and shepherdesses, the sighing-singing lovers with their cruel-fair mistresses were pasteboard figures which the poets had to move around gracefully. And the Elizabethan poet wrote for an audience as sophisticated in literary matters as he himself was. The medieval poet, on the other hand, was concerned more with ultimate than with imaginative reality; he was troubled by man's relationship to God and his difficult task of taking up his cross and following Jesus Christ. The medieval poet was more didactic, if you will—but *didactic* does not characterize his poetry as well as *devotional,* which at least conveys something of its emotional fervor.* His devotion, however, was to something more important and more real than his Elizabethan counterpart's supposed devotion to a mistress. And his audience was more popular than courtly. Yet along with—or in spite of—his devotional purpose, the medieval poet produced "For ou þat is so feir ant brist," "Adam lay I-bowndyn," "Somer is comen & winter gon," "Wanne mine eyhnen misten," "That lovely lady sat and song," "A child is boren amonges man," and a host of other lyrics full of charm—which is the nature of the Elizabethan as well as of the medieval song.

But the Elizabethan song is more sophisticated; or perhaps it is merely more sophisticated more often. It employs techniques which the medieval religious song rarely—if ever—uses. The Elizabethan air, for instance, may pit a complex variation against its basic metrical pattern, and repeat exactly this total structure of pattern and variation from stanza to stanza. The madrigal may repeat and vary special "sense-phrases" which slow down its basic metrical pattern; it also varies its line lengths —often abruptly—and usually does not rime them in a strict order of couplets or alternate quatrains.[2] The medieval song, however, exudes its own kind of sophis-

* Some religious lyrics are more concerned with the inculcation of moral truths than with the typical Franciscan attempt to elicit emotional response. Such is the dreary series of refrain poems in the Vernon MS, which Brown prints almost entire (Nos. 95–120).

tication in its modulation of rimes, its aureate diction, and its alliterative patterns. The modulation of rimes is best exhibited in polystrophic structure, where one stanza form counterpoints another, as in "Ar ne kuthe ich sorghe non" and "Haill! Glaid and glorius." Somewhat analogous in the carol is the relationship between stanza and burden; the burden may echo, modify, or ignore the diction, line length, and rime of the stanza.* The aureate diction of many fifteenth-century religious lyrics still betrays its sophistication, although it has lost its glitter over the years. Dunbar's ballade in praise of Mary is a tour de force—but a very sophisticated one, as not only its diction, but its handling of the address-plus-petition formula, its alliteration, consonance, and assonance readily attest. The trouble with much of this courtly poetry is that it is too self-conscious; the Elizabethan lyric is often just as self-conscious, but somehow its sophistication seems more natural. The religious subject matter of the medieval song adapts itself less willingly to such ostentation. The third area of sophistication in the earlier song lies in its pattern of alliteration, which often combines with consonance and assonance. Not only Dunbar and fifteenth-century poets generally, but poets in the fourteenth and thirteenth centuries make their songs glisten with these devices. The modern reader may have to train his ear to catch the sometimes elaborate patterning. He is very likely to skip over poems like "Haile be þu, mari, maiden bright" (XIV, No. 31), yet the poem rewards careful listening. At times the sound is structural, tying together two lines which do not rime, as the italicized consonance, assonance, and alliteration do in the following lines:

18   *Al* h*i*s w*il* *it* *sal* be wroght
         in h*i*s an*cele*.

---

* The burden of "Vppon the cros nailid I was for the" (Greene, No. 263a) contrasts sharply with the stanzas in tone as well as sound. Its phrasing, moreover, approximates that of the dramatic lyric.

Notice the alliterative cross-patterning in the following:

>   Þe king was riche, þe gold was rede,
> 32   Þe reclis fel til his goddhed.

A more elaborate patterning occurs in the use of the *s, l,* and *v* sounds in the second stanza:

>   Mi sinful saule sighes sare;
>   Liued i haue in sin and care,
> 8   Leue i wil and do na mare.
>   mi leuedi fre,
>   Saul and bodi, lijf and dede, bi-teche i þe.

At other times the sound ties together two halves of a line; line 48 is very reminiscent of classical Old English alliterative verse:

>   Leuedi mari,   moder o liue.

But not only does the alliteration cross-pattern, the consonant sequence *l v d m r* in the first half rearranges to become *m d r l v* in the second. Coincidental? Perhaps. The poem as a whole is thus characterized by its coincidences.* The medieval song does not always jog merrily along its metrical way. Although it is seldom as ostentatious as the Elizabethan lyric, it can match in its own way the sophistication of any group of English songs.

The Elizabethan song, unlike its less luminous medieval counterpart, can dazzle, not only by its techniques of sound, but also by its imagery. Its diction is sensu-

---

* "Heʒe Louerd, þou here my bone" (Brook, No. 13; XIV, No. 6) is another excellent example of sophisticated lyric. As we have noted earlier, it alternates its stanza form, the shorter stanza repeating the rime scheme (but not the rime) of the last five lines of the longer stanza. Each line alliterates, and sometimes the alliteration ties together stanzas not tied by concatenation. The pattern of alliteration, consonance, and assonance is often as complex as in lines 2–3:

>   þat madest middelert ant mone,
>   ant mon of murþes munne.

ous, pretty, rich, lush. The pastoral poets sported with Amaryllis in pastel shades; the Ovidian poets used dark reds and purples. The medieval poet, to begin with, had fewer words at his command; even Chaucer complained of the difficulty of composing in English. And there is no medieval Spenser. True, the lushness of the Elizabethans is foreshadowed in late medieval courtly narrative, but scarcely so in the lyric. The Elizabethans also lavished figurative imagery on their poems. Not so the medievals. Thomas of Hales and the author of "In a valey of þis restles mynde" represent that small proportion of poets, mostly courtly, who utilized a structure of multiple images. The Elizabethans, spurred by Petrarch, theoretically used their images to express the emotional state of their speakers; the medievals used their religious images to penetrate reality. They were not concerned with sensuous appeal. Their imagery expresses the suprasensible reality which underlies it, as the figurative epithets and allegories like "On Cristes day, I vnderstond" (Greene, No. 321) so uncompromisingly demonstrate. Finally, like the Elizabethan imagery drawn from Petrarch, medieval religious imagery is thoroughly traditional. But the unity of existence, which so characterizes medieval thought, and which is reflected in the imagery, begins to crumble in the Renaissance. The images begin to lose their insight into reality and become instead mere poetic trinkets.

As we have been noting all along, the Elizabethan and the medieval song differ in their subject matter. This is obvious. It is also significant. To assess the place of the medieval religious lyric in English poetry means we must compare it with others of its type. It compares favorably with Elizabethan song, but the latter is not outstandingly religious. To what body of religious poetry may we then compare it? Certainly not to Donne's poems, for Donne bases his poetic rhythms on the rhythm of actual conversation. His are dramatic lyrics, not songs, and to contrast the medieval religious lyric with the dramatic lyric is to fall into the same mistaken evaluation that is already rampant. Hopkins and Eliot we must also eliminate for the same reason. Some of Herbert's lyrics are songs; the best Middle English religious lyrics equal and sometimes surpass them. But where else can we find the charm, the technique, the emotion, the vitality of the Middle English religious lyrics? Where else can we find the wit? Not in Isaac Watts.* Not in Charles Wesley,† nor in other eighteenth-century hymn writers. Certainly not in the nineteenth and early twentieth centuries, which collected their endeavors under such revealing titles as *At the Beautiful Gate, Lyra Apostolica, Songs of Zion, Unto the Desired Haven, The Uplands of God, Sabbath Bells, At the Evening Time, Cheering Words for the Master's Workers.* Twentieth-century hymnals disclose such promising titles as "Who Is on the Lord's Side?" "Jesus, Savior, Pilot Me," "Why Not Now?" "Will Jesus Find Us Watching?" "Crimson Calvary Answers, 'No!'" "Tell Mother I'll Be There." These saccharine morsels should be cast into some aesthetic limbo. The melody of the Middle English religious lyric is more like what one should hope to hear in Paradise.

* Alas, and did my Saviour bleed?
    And did my Sov'reign die?
  Would He devote that sacred head
    For such a worm as I?

† Come, almighty to deliver,
    Let us all thy grace receive;
  Suddenly return, and never,
    Never more thy temples leave.
  Thee we would be always blessing,
    Serve thee as thy hosts above,
  Pray and praise thee without ceasing,
    Glory in thy perfect love.

1. Catherine Ing, *Elizabethan Lyrics*, p. 21, cited above in the Preface; Hallett Smith, *Elizabethan Poetry* (Harvard, 1952), p. 267.
2. Ing, pp. 128–129, 135.

APPENDIX

"HEƷE LOUERD, ÞOU HERE MY BONE"

Heʒe Louerd, þou here my bone,   *prayer*
þat madest middelert ant mone,   *earth and moon*
ant mon of murþes munne.   *man*   *to bear in mind*
4 Trusti kyng ant trewe in trone,
þat þou be wiþ me sahte sone,   *reconciled*
asoyle me of sunne.   *absolve*
ffol ich wes, in folies   *fool*   *rejoicing in my folly*
  fayn;
8 in luthere lastes y am layn;   *hateful*   *sins*
þat makeþ myn þryftes þunne,   *gains*   *thin*
þat semly sawes wes woned to seyn.   *accustomed*
Nou is marred al my meyn,   *strength*
12   away is al my wunne.   *joy*

Vnwunne haueþ myn wonges wet,   *cheeks*
þat makeþ me rouþes rede.   *lamentations utter*
Ne sem y nout þer y am set: *suit*   *wherever*
16 þer me calleþ me fulle-flet   *they call me fill-floor*
ant waynoun   *good-for-nothing man-*
  wayteglede.   *who-sits-gazing-at-the-fire*

Whil ich wes in wille   *formerly*   *lust's*
  wolde,   *domination*
in vch a bour among þe bolde
  yholde wiþ þe heste;   *upheld command*
nou y may no fynger folde,
lutel loued ant lasse ytolde,   *regarded*
  yleued wiþ þe leste.   *left*

24 A goute me haþ ygreyþed so   *affected*
 ant oþer eueles monye mo,
  y not whet bote is beste.   *remedy*
 Þar er wes wilde ase þe ro *where formerly I* *roe*
28 nou y swyke, y mei nout so,   *leave off*
  hit siweþ me so faste.   *follows* *intently*

 ffaste y wes on horse heh   *vigorous*
  ant werede worly wede;   *costly garments*
32 nou is faren al my feh,   *gone* *property*
 wiþ serewe þat ich hit euer seh;   *saw*
  a staf ys nou my stede.   *steed*

 When y se steden styþe in stalle *steeds* *strong*
36 ant y go haltinde in þe halle,   *limping*
  myn huerte gynneþ to helde.   *sink*
 Þat er wes wildest inwiþ walle   *within*
 nou is vnder fote yfalle
40 ant mey no fynger felde.
 Þer ich wes luef, icham ful loht, *dear* *hateful*
 ant alle myn godes me atgoht,   *depart*
  myn gomenes waxeþ gelde. *pleasures* *barren*
44 Þat feyre founden me mete ant *those who kindly*
  cloht,   *provided*
 hue wrieþ awey as hue were   *turn*
  wroht—   *angry*
  such is euel ant elde.

 Euel ant elde ant oþer wo
48 foleweþ me so faste
 me þunkeþ myn herte brekeþ atuo.   *in two*
 Suete God, whi shal hit swo?
  Hou mai hit lengore laste?

52 Whil mi lif wes luþer ant *formerly* *wicked*
  lees;   *false*
 Glotonie mi glemon wes,   *minstrel*
  wiþ me he wonede a while;   *lived*
 Prude wes my plowe-fere,   *playfellow*
56 Lecherie my lauendere— *laundress* (i.e., *mistress*)

wiþ hem is gabbe ant gyle.	*falsehood guile*
Coueytise myn keyes bere,	
Niþe ant Onde were mi fere,	*Hatred and Envy companions*
þat bueþ folkes fyle;	*are vile*
Lyare wes mi latymer,	*interpreter*
Sleuthe ant Slep mi bedyuer,	*bedfellows*
þat weneþ me vmbe while.	*pleased at times*

64	Vmbe while y am to wene,	*to be pleased*
	when y shal murþes meten.	*encounter*
	Monne mest y am to mene;	*pity*
	Lord, þat hast me lyf to lene,	*grant*
	such lotes lef me leten.	*behavior abandon*

	Such lyf ich haue lad fol ȝore.	
	Merci, Louerd, y nul namore;	
	bowen ichulle to bete.	*atone*
72	Syker hit siweþ me ful sore,	*truly*
	gabbes les ant luþere lore;	*lies untrue wicked advice*
	sunnes bueþ vnsete.	*sins are evil*
	Godes heste ne huld y noht,	*command*
76	bote euer aȝeyn is wille y wroht;	*against His will*
	mon lereþ me to lete.	*they taught me to leave off*
	Such serewe haþ myn sides þurhsoht	*pierced*
	þat al y weolewe away to noht	*wither*
80	when y shal murþes mete.	

	To mete murþes ich wes wel fous	*eager*
	ant comely mon ta calle	
	(y sugge by oþer ase bi ous)	*say*
84	alse ys hirmon halt in hous,	*as is servant haughty*
	ase heued-hount in halle.	*head-hound*

	Dredful deþ, why wolt þou dare?	*lie motionless*
	Bryng þis body þat is so bare	
	ant yn bale ybounde.	

Careful mon ycast in care,
y falewe as flour ylet forþfare,   *wither*   *left to die*
   ychabbe myn deþes wounde.

92 Murþes helpeþ me no more;
help me, Lord, er þen ich hore,   *before I turn gray*
   ant stunt my lyf a stounde. *put an end to*   *in time*
þat ʒokkyn haþ yʒyrned   *he who desire*   *longed for*
   ʒore,   *for long*

96 nou hit sereweþ him ful sore,
   ant bringeþ him to grounde.

To grounde hit haueþ him ybroht;
   whet ys þe beste bote

100 bote heryen him þat haht vs boht,   *praise*
vre Lord þat al þis world haþ
      wroht,
   ant fallen him to fote? *humble oneself before Him*

Nou ich am to deþe ydyht,   *ready*

104   ydon is al my dede.
God vs lene of ys lyht   *grant*
þat we of sontes habben syht   *saints*
   ant heuene to mede! Amen.   *as reward*

STABAT IUXTA CHRISTI CRUCEM

1a. Stabat juxta Christi
    crucem,
    Stabat videns vitae du-
    cem
    Vitae valefacere,

1b. Stabat mater nec jam
    mater,
    Et quid sit eventus ater,
    Novo novit funere.

2a. Stabat virgo spectans
    crucem
    Et utramque pati lucem,
    Sed plus suam doluit,

2b. Ista stabat, hic pende-
    bat,
    Et quod foris hic fere-
    bat,
    Intus haec sustinuit.

3a. Intus cruci conclavatur,
    Intus sui jugulatur
    Mater agni gladio,

3b. Intus martyr consecra-
    tur,
    Intus tota concrematur
    Amoris incendio.

4a. Modo manus, modo la-
    tus,
    Modo ferro pes foratus
    Oculis resumitur,

4b. Modo caput spinis tu-
    tum,
    Cujus orbis totus nutum
    Et sentit et sequitur.

5a. Os verendum litum spu-
    tis
    Et flagellis rupta cutis
    Et tot rivi sanguinis,

5b. Probra, risus et quae
    restant,
    Orbitati tela praestant
    Et dolori virginis.

6a. Tempus nacta trux na-
    tura

6b. Nunc extorquet cum
    usura

Nunc exposcit sua jura, Gemitus, quos paritura
Nunc dolores acuit,   Naturae detinuit.

7a. Nunc, nunc parit, nunc 7b. Nunc se dolor orbitati
   scit vere,   Dilatus in partu nati
  Quam maternum sit do-   Praesentat in funere.
   lere,
   Quam amarum pa-
   rere,

8a. Nunc fit mater, sed do- 8b. Nam pudicos gestus fo-
   loris,   ris
  Servat tamen hic pudo- Non deflorat vis doloris
   ris   Intus urens anxiam.
   Virginalis gratiam,

9a. Triduanus ergo fletus 9b. Laeta lucet spes dolenti,
  Laeta demum est dele- Leto namque resurgenti
   tus   Conresurgunt omnia.
   Surgentis victoria,

10a. Christi novus hic nata- 10b. Hinc processit, hinc sur-
   lis   rexit,
  Formam partus virgina- Hinc et inde Christus
   lis   exit
   Clauso servat tumulo,   Intacto signaculo.

11a. Eja mater, eja laeta, 11b. Nostrae quoque laetum
  Fletus tui nox expleta   mane
   Lucescit in gaudium, Nocti plus quam tridu-
         anae
        Tuum redde filium.

INDEX OF POEMS

INDEX OF POEMS AND AUTHORS

Poems are listed by first lines; authors are Middle English.

"A child is boren a-monges man," 28, 31, 172

"A Mayde cristes me bit yorne," 122-124

"Adam lay I-bowndyn," 6-7, 32n., 172

"Ar ne kuthe ich sorghe non," 28, 30, 173

"Ase y me rod þis ender day," 74

"At a sprynge wel vnder a þorn," 4n.

"Blodles & bonles," 145

"Crist makiþ to man a fair present," 27, 146-150

"Cristes milde moder, seynte marie," 94-96

Dunbar, William, 63, 173

"Edi beo þu, heuene quene," 97-100, 144

"Fadur and sone & holy gost," 41

"For ou þat is so feir ant brist," 126-131, 172

"Ful feir flour is þe lilie," 113-114

"Glade us, maiden," 74

"Haile be þu, mari, maiden bright," 75-77, 94, 173-174

"Haill! Glaid and glorius," 27-28, 30, 173

"Hale, sterne superne," 63-64

"Hayl mari! hic am sori," 41

"He bare hym vp, he bare hym down," 115-118

"He yaf him self as good felawe," 121-122

Herebert, William, 118

"Herodes, þou wykked fo," 118-120, 132

"Heʒe Louerd, þou here my bone," 29-30, 51-54, 174, 179-182

"Hostis Herodis impie," 118

"Hyt semes quite and is red," 140

"I haue laborede sore," 45-46

"I saw a fayr maydyn," 26

"I sayh hym wiþ ffless al bi-sprad," 19-21

"I Syng of a myden," 158-167

"Iesu Crist, heouene kyng," 43

"Iesu cristes milde moder," 89n., 144

"Iesu dulcis memoria," 39

"Iesu, suete is þe loue of þe," 39-40

"Iesus, þat wald efter midnight," 73

"Ihesu lorde, þat madest me," 57

"Ihesu, that alle this worlde hast wroghte," 73-74

"Ihesu, þat alle þis worlde hast wroȝt," 111n.

"In a valey of þis restles mynde," 59-62, 84, 175

"In place as man may se," 139-140

"Kyndeli is now mi coming," 14-15

"Kyrieleyson, haue mercy, good lorde," 64

"Ler to louen as i loue þe," 48-49

"Leuedi sainte marie, moder and meide," 10-11, 42, 142-143

"Loue me brouthte," 5-6, 32

"Louerd, þu clepedest me," 36-38

"Luf es lyf þat lastes ay," 58

"Lullay, lullay, litel child," 24-25 (carol), 141

Lydgate, John, 139

"Lystne, man, lystne to me," 44-45

"Man and wyman, loket to me," 72n.

"Marie moder, wel the be," 57

"Mary, moder of mercy & pyte," 64

"Marye, mayde, mylde and fre," 65-72

"Merci abid an loke al day," 72n.

"Nou goth sonne vnder wod," 80-83, 84, 105

"Nou skrinkeþ rose ant lylieflour," 97, 100-105

"Nv yh she blostme sprynge," 22-23

"O Ihesu, lett me neuer forgett thy byttur passion," 9-10

"Of on þat is so fayr and briȝt," 8-9, 131n. See also "For ou þat is so feir ant brist"

"Off alle women þat euer were borne," 47-48

"On Cristes day, I vnderstond," 112-113, 175

"Out of your slepe aryse and wake," 143-144

"Quanne hic se on rode," 142

Richard de Caistre, 57

Rolle, Richard, 58-59

Ryman, James, 140n.

"Seinte marie, leuedi brist," 74

"Seinte marie, moder milde," 43

"Somer is comen & winter gon," 25-26, 114-115, 133, 172

"Stabat iuxta Christi crucem," 150, 183-184

"Stond wel, moder, vnder rode," 11n., 77-80

"Swete ihesu, king of blisse," 63

"Þat leueli leor wid spald ischent," 150-154

"That lovely lady sat and song," 49-50, 172

"Þe fader of heuene," 11n., 26-27

"The fyrste joye, as I you telle," 74

"The fyrst day wan Crist was borne," 12, 32

"Þe minde of þi passiun," 13-14, 80

"The sunne of grace hym schynit in," 23-24

"The ten comawndementis I haue broke," 40

"Ther is no rose of swych vertu," 155-158

Thomas of Hales, 122, 124, 132, 175

"Vndo þi dore, my spuse dere," 125-126

"Vppon the cros nailid I was for the," 173n.

"Wanne mine eyhnen misten," 15-17, 172

"When þi hed whaketh," 17-19

William of Shoreham, 65, 69, 71

"Wynter wakeneþ al my care," 105-106, 133

"Ʒe þat pasen be þe weyʒe," 45

INDEX OF PRINCIPAL TOPICS

INDEX OF PRINCIPAL TOPICS

Address plus petition, 62-72, 77, 83, 84, 173

Addressee, 42-44, 47, 49, 51, 53

Allegory, 109-118, 120, 135n.; literal level, 109, 110, 112; allegorical level, 109; moral (tropological) level, 109; anagogical level, 30, 109. *See also* Symbol

Analogy, 20, 21, 90-106 *passim*, 109-111, 132

Audience, medieval, viii, ix, 15, 31, 35, 40, 41, 45, 50-51, 58, 84, 139, 144, 172

Confession, formula for, 18, 41, 42, 52, 56

Dramatic lyric, ix, x, 3, 9-11, 22, 32, 35-55 *passim*, 138, 173n.

Elizabethan lyric, viii, 171-176

Existence, unity of, 92-106 *passim*, 131, 132, 133

Form, mechanic and organic, 56-57, 83, 84

Franciscan school of poetry, 47, 49, 51, 78, 81, 107, 140-142, 172n.

French influence, 94, 97, 98, 100, 102

Genres: carol, 25, 26, 154; *débat*, 77; *descort*, 14, 15; figurative eulogy, 68; lullaby carol, 49; *pastourelle*, 100, 102, 103, 105, 134n. *See also Topoi*

Imagery, viii, x, 9, 30, 39, 45, 84, 106-133, 145-167 *passim*, 171, 175. *See also* Allegory; Symbol

Jesus Christ: as addressee, 42-43, 47; as speaker, 6, 44-46, 50, 59

Litany of the Saints, 19, 64

Lyric situation, ix, 9, 32, 34-55

Mary: as addressee, 42-43, 84; as speaker, 46-50, 79-80

Meditation, 59, 60, 72-80, 83

Music, 9, 11-12, 14, 21, 24, 30, 34n.; as lyric quality, 3, 4, 7, 13, 32n., 64

Mysticism, 38-40, 57-62, 126

Rhetorical poetry, 107-108, 109, 124

Secular influence. *See* French influence; Troubadour poetry

Sermons, poetry in, 44-45

Sinner, as speaker, 40-44, 50-54, 56, 68, 84

Song, vii-x, 3-32, 35-36, 40, 44, 51, 54, 69, 84, 106, 108, 133, 138-139, 171-176

Sound structures: linear, 13-21, 83, 120; monostrophic, 13, 21-26, 30, 40; polystrophic, 13, 26-30

Speaker, characterization of, 12, 28, 30, 35-54 *passim*, 80

Symbol, 109-112, 118-120. *See also* Allegory

Tone, 22-23, 33-34n., 64, 92-94

Topoi: appeals from the cross, 44-45, 46; five joys of Mary, 74-77; hours of the cross, 73; Marian laments, 46-48; signs of death, 15-19, 32

Troubadour poetry, 92-94, 100

Wit, poetry of, 138-167

A NOTE ABOUT THE AUTHOR

STEPHEN JOSEPH MANNING was born in Indiana, Pennsylvania, in 1930. He received his A.B. degree *magna cum laude* from Catholic University of America in 1952 and his Ph.D. four years later from The Johns Hopkins University. He has been a member of the faculty at the University of Colorado and is at present Assistant Professor of English at the University of Virginia. Professor Manning's articles have appeared in *PMLA, Comparative Literature, Journal of English and Germanic Philology, Modern Language Notes, The Explicator,* and *ELH.*

DATE DUE

JY 7 '65			
GAYLORD			PRINTED IN U.S.A.